Productivity Improvement
A Guide for
Small Business

Productivity Improvement
A Guide for
Small Business

Ira B. Gregerman

An Inc./Van Nostrand Reinhold Publication

VAN NOSTRAND REINHOLD COMPANY
NEW YORK CINCINNATI TORONTO LONDON MELBOURNE

Copyright © 1984 by Inc. Publishing Corporation

Library of Congress Catalog Card Number: 83-23444

ISBN: 0-442-22968-2

Manufactured in the United States of America

Published by Van Nostrand Reinhold Publishing
135 West 50th Street, New York, N.Y. 10020

Van Nostrand Reinhold
480 Latrobe Street
Melbourne, Victoria 3000, Australia

Van Nostrand Reinhold Company Limited
Molly Millars Lane
Wokingham, Berkshire, England

Macmillan of Canada
Division of Gage Publishing Limited
164 Commander Boulevard
Agincourt, Ontario M1S 3C7, Canada

15 14 13 12 11 10 9 8 7 6 5 4 3 2 1

Library of Congress Cataloging in Publication Data

Gregerman, Ira B., 1937–
  Productivity improvement.

  Bibliography: p.
  Includes index.
  1. Labor productivity. 2. Small business — Management.
I. Title.
HD57.G685   1983   658.3'14   83-23444
ISBN 0-442-22968-2

Contents

Preface

Every manager faces three types of problems:

- Those which they can do nothing about and with which they must learn to *cope*.

- Those which someone else must solve and for which they must *influence* the solution.

- Those which they can resolve and on which they must take *action*.

Productivity improvement and this book deal with the last two categories. The first one (containing government regulations, interest rates, inflation, and so on) will be essentially ignored. Why waste valuable time playing Don Quixote? If you, the reader, are typical of the smaller business entrepreneur or larger business managers, you are interested in the *bottom line* impact of productivity improvement.

Your answer to the question, "Would you like to increase your profits after taxes by 25 percent without increasing sales, fixed assets, debt, or labor?" should be a resounding YES! This can be done by productivity improvement. Let's look at an example. Consider the following financial data of a business:

1980 Income Statement

Sales	$25,000,000
Cost of Sales	16,250,000
Gross Profit	8,750,000
Depreciation and Other Expenses	6,346,000
Profit from Operations	2,404,000
Income Taxes	1,154,000
Net Profit	$ 1,250,000

To substantially increase after-tax profits—say by 25 percent to $1,562,500—would require a 25-percent increase in sales to $31,250,000. This illustration, of course, assumes that expenses and taxes would stay at the same rate. The same profit gain, however, can be achieved by productivity increases. For example, the $312,500 increase in profits could be achieved by reducing the cost of sales by only 3.7 percent. In fact, a 15-percent reduction in cost of sales would double after-tax profits. This example, simple though it may be, demonstrates the bottom-line impact of productivity improvement.

The other illustrations in this book are not so simple. I have either presented them from true situations or constructed them to demonstrate certain concepts and points. Company names in most cases are fictitious and the data have been adjusted. I am sure a few readers will test my mathematical prowess by duplicating the calculations in the measurement chapter. Should you find some slight differences, they are caused by rounding off numbers for simplicity.

To cash in on the benefits of productivity improvement, an organization needs to look at changing the way some things are done—planning, communications, resource utilization, top management commitment, training, employee attitudes, measurement responsibility, and of course improvement techniques themselves. To accomplish this, productivity improvement should be closely linked to the organization's long-range strategic planning process. There are no shortcuts, no magic formulas, and no handbooks with the answers. To think otherwise is foolhardy. Many organizations that are trying to overcome twenty years of neglect are finding this out. Buying a consultant's "green pill" is not the answer. A change of attitude, a recognition of the role management plays in creating the problem, an admission to the sacrifice we have been making toward long-term corporate health are the kinds of pills we need to take. Only then can we begin to treat the problem right. It is akin to a physician prescribing medication without a diagnosis. The result is malpractice or malmanagement.

Many companies have discovered this and have taken appropriate actions to turn things around. But it's slow—it takes a lot more energy to turn a battleship than a row boat. This book will deal with some of the ways this can be accomplished and some of the techniques that have been successful. Perhaps an appropriate caveat would be: "Make sure you *adapt* the ideas and techniques to be discussed—never *adopt* them."

Acknowledgments

This book would not be complete without acknowledging those people who have contributed to its preparation. I extend my sincere appreciation and thanks:

To the many organizations with whom I have worked as an employee or consultant for real-world exposure to what productivity improvement is all about.

To the hundreds of managers and executives who attended American Productivity Center seminars I conducted and who were willing to share their stories, experiences, and opinions.

To the members and officers of the American Productivity Management Association for openly sharing information about the management of productivity strategies.

To the American Productivity Center and its staff for the opportunity of serving them as an Associate in 1979 and obtaining the fundamental foundations needed to understand the reasons why productivity-improvement strategies succeed or fail.

My last and most important acknowledgement can never be adequate—my family, whom I love more than life itself:

Minna

Daniel

Rhonda

Jason

Productivity Improvement
A Guide for
Small Business

*Equally important to restoring economic stability in America is improvement of our rate of productivity growth. Increasing productivity is the only way we can elevate our standard of living. For most of the history of our country productivity has increased, resulting in an increasing standard of living, expressed in higher pay, better working conditions and more leisure time. At present, however, our productivity is not increasing. Our machines and factories are old and wearing out. If we no longer have increases in productivity, we will have less wealth for culture, for education, for religion and medicine. As our productivity goes down, our living standard also will have to move down and our prices will move up.** *

—Jay Van Andel, Chairman of the Board, Amway Corporation

*Source: *Imprimis,* Ronald L. Trowbridge, ed., vol. 10, no. 6 (Hillsdale, Michigan: Hillsdale College, June 1981). Copyright © 1981 by Hillsdale College.

Yes, Virginia, There Is a Productivity Problem

Introduction

It is almost impossible to pick up a newspaper or trade magazine and not find at least one reference to productivity in the editorial content or advertisements. Productivity is receiving much attention because of its effect on many important elements of our national economy. From the mid-1940s to the mid-1960s, our nation's productivity grew at about 3.2% per year. After the mid-1960s, growth declined to an annual rate of 1.5% per year. This data is shown graphically in Figure 1.1. To make matters worse, the most recent data for 1980 and 1981 show a continuous negative growth rate comparable to 1979's 1.0% decline. Someone once estimated the dollar value of the decline in productivity as being equal to the sum of the national defense budget, plus the national welfare costs, plus $100 cash for every person in the United States—about $200 billion. This inability to maintain our productivity growth rate has contributed significantly to:

- A slowing of our economic growth,
- Preparing a path for increasing foreign competition,
- Adding to already increasing production costs,
- Erosion of real wages and profits, and
- Increasing the cost of capital and research and development.

These may appear to be distant national problems to most, and not directly related to everyday business activities, but they

FIGURE **1.1.**

Output Per Hour Worked in the Private Business Sector Between 1950 and 1980.

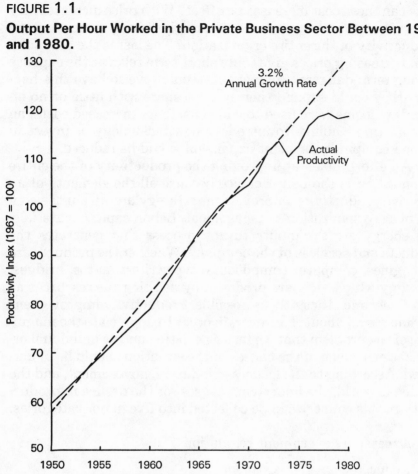

Source: U.S. Bureau of Labor Statistics.

are. The effects can be felt in a number of ways. Consider the increasing business pressures such as:

- Wages that continue to increase without offsetting productivity increases,

- Pension and fringe benefit costs that keep skyrocketing,

- Demands for reduced work hours,

- Ever-advancing energy costs,

- Escalating indirect white-collar and professional worker costs, and

- A decided shift in the needs and attitudes of the workforce.

How can these cost increases be offset? With price increases? By absorbing them through declining margins? Or by increasing the productivity of the entire organization? The last is the best solution. Increasing prices gives only short-term relief at the expense of long-term dangers. Competitors would love to have this happen—they could expand their market share with little or no effort. If margins were used to compensate for increased costs, an organization's ability to introduce new technology or invest in needed equipment or plant expansion would be reduced.

An effort aimed at improving the productivity of the entire organization is the better choice because all the elements of an effective productivity-improvement strategy are within the control of the organization's management. Labor, capital, materials, and energy are the inputs to any process that generates the products and services of the company. Whether the products are jet engines, computer components, typewriters, autos, bridges, or buggy whips, they are produced by utilizing the resources as effectively and efficiently as possible. Productivity improvement is what it's all about. However, in order to appreciate the magnitude of the problem that we face as a nation and as individual organizations, some of the causes of the situation should be understood. According to the leaders of industry, government, and the academic world, the underlying causes for the decline in productivity in this country can be collected into five major categories:

1. Excessive government regulations.

2. Reduced capital investment.

3. Diluted research and development expenditures.

4. Exploding energy costs.

5. Human resource changes.

Before we venture into each of these, it would be beneficial to look at some definitions of productivity.

Productivity Defined

Productivity in its simplest form is a ratio of the products and services of an organization to the inputs consumed to generate them. Looked at a little differently, it is a measure of the efficient use of a company's resources. For the mathematically oriented:

$$\text{Productivity} = \frac{\text{Total Outputs of the Firm}}{\text{Total Inputs Used by the Firm}}$$

Thus if a company generates the same output with less input, the ratio gets larger and it can be said that the organization has been more productive. This increase then is at the heart of productivity-improvement efforts. It is insufficient to measure the ratio of output to input unless something is done to increase that ratio over time. To do this, management and the organization as a whole have only five options to making the ratio bigger.

1. Make the output larger for the same input.

2. Make the input smaller for the same output.

3. Increase the output while decreasing the input.

4. Increase output faster than the input increases.

5. Decrease the output less than the inputs decrease.

The following representations may help to visualize these five possibilities:

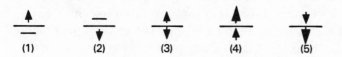

Some examples of these alternatives will further help to clarify the concept that we will deal with in much greater detail as this book unfolds.

In condition (*3*) we have the ideal situation: getting more out with less input. Expanding markets coupled with new technologies in manufacturing (or new materials or new processes) will provide this type of result. Take the case of computer manufacturers who are experiencing increasing demand for hardware and new computer applications at a time when the internal architecture is advancing by leaps and bounds. The introduction of computer technology to the service sector has assisted that portion of the economy to expand. The result is what is seen in the third alternative—more out with less in.

The first fraction might represent a condition where effective lowering of scrap losses has enabled a steel mill to generate more "usable" steel while still employing the same resources. Similarly, a concerted effort to improve quality, thus reducing recycles or "do overs," results in more out the door for the same use of labor, capital, materials, and energy. The alternative represented by the second situation is typical of effective cost-reduction programs. However, cost-reduction programs have a tendency to revert back to the original state of being if not continually nurtured and promoted. A large infusion of automated equipment would also fall into category (2). This is especially true if it substantially reduced the use of one or more of the other resources. Robots introduced into the automobile assembly lines of Japan and now the United States will substantially reduce the need for manual labor in welding and painting operations. The result may be more cars, but the aim is to use less input to generate the equivalent number of units.

The fourth alternative typifies the introduction of new products or the start up of a new facility. Output goes up as does input; however, the rates are different. On the flip side of this alternative is the situation that is represented by condition (5) —representing the closing of a plant or the elimination of a product.

Therefore, it should now be apparent that to measure productivity requires only the establishment of outputs and inputs, dividing one by the other and tracking the changes over time. There are only two problems with this—one is the output and the other the input. Combining the various outputs and inputs gives most measurers a great deal of difficulty. Accounting for variations in quality, labor intensity, combining energy forms for heating, lighting, and transportation are just a few of the examples that make the subject difficult but not impossible. It is well worth the time and effort to understand the basics of productivity measurement for the organization as a whole and for the various subgroups. The subject of productivity measurement will be handled in detail in Chapter II.

Government Regulations

In 1923 there were 175 different government agencies. Today, there are over 400. The cost of this growth has swollen regulatory budgets from $2.2 billion in 1974 to $4.8 billion in 1979.

Chase Manhattan reports estimate that the cost of federal regulation—administration, enforcement, and compliance—exceeds $100 billion annually. More than 80 federal agencies regulate our business activity and the Code of Federal Regulations now runs to some 70,000 pages. In some industries, the heads of research report that they spend more time filling out government reports than doing research.

In 1978, General Motors employed over 25,000 people to ensure that it complied with government regulations. This translates into nearly $2 billion, or about $700.00 in added cost to the average GM automobile. As if that weren't enough, consider that there might be at least an equal number of government employees that are reading, filing, and in other ways working with the data. An executive of General Motors once observed, "We're glad that we don't get all the help from the government that we are paying for."

A recent study of the costs associated with government regulations pointed out the following:

> The Lord's prayer contains 56 words, Lincoln's Gettysburg Address is 268 words, and the Declaration of Independence is 1,322 words, but a government regulation on the sale of cabbage requires 26,911 words.*

And from other sources come some equally interesting notes:

- Roy Ash, former director of the Office of Management and Budget, estimates that the Environmental Protection Agency's regulatory efforts have increased the inflation rate between 2% and 3%.

- Armco, Inc., was required to install scrubbing equipment at one of its plants. The scrubber filters out 21.2 pounds of iron oxide dust per hour. But electricity needed to run the 1,020 HP motor will generate 23 pounds of sulphur, nitrogen oxide, and other gaseous materials. A net gain of 1.8 pounds of pollutants is placed into the environment each hour.

- The Department of Transportation was pushing Vale, Colorado's transit system into equipping 14 buses with wheelchair lifts. At first blush this is a noble gesture—until

---

*"Cost of Government Regulation Study," Arthur Anderson & Co., March 1979.

you dig a little deeper and find that there is only one wheel-chair user in the entire system. When asked about the specially equipped buses, the handicapped person is reported to have indicated that he wouldn't take the bus anyway!

- Fifty years ago, ground was broken for the Empire State Building. In just 410 days the first tenant moved in. It is not difficult to believe the estimates that today the same project would take over 3½ years.

Abraham Lincoln had an observation that applies to our concern over excessive regulations:

You cannot strengthen the weak by weakening the strong.
You cannot help small men by tearing down big men.
You cannot help the poor by destroying the rich.
You cannot help the wage earner by pulling down the wage payer.
You cannot further the brotherhood of man by inciting class hatreds.
You cannot establish security on borrowed money.
You cannot build character and courage by taking away a man's independence.
You cannot help men permanently by doing for them what they could do for themselves.

Capital Investment

In its 1979 Annual Report, The Council of Economic Advisors pointed out that, "Only by devoting a significant share of current products to replace, modernize and expand the capital stock can we hope to maintain adequate growth and productivity." Perhaps the Council should have added to this statement the need for increased capital availability for business in general.

This need comes from the realization that we must cope with an ever-increasing foreign presence in our domestic markets. Of all our major international competitors, Japan and Germany have the highest investment ratios of capital to Gross National Product. Since 1960, Japan has invested in fixed capital at the rate of 30% of its GNP. Germany and France have investment rates of 25% and 22% respectively. The United States is a distant fourth with a mere 14%. One of the causes for this is found in the personal-savings rates of the workers in these countries. In 1979, average Japanese workers saved 20% of their disposable income. German and French workers put away 14% and 16%, whereas in the United States the average savings rate was only 4%. The reason for these disparities in rates between the United States and its competitors rests simply in the incentives provided by the tax structures that encourage or discourage saving. The importance of these savings is easy to understand. As savings increase, more cash is available for institutions to lend to businesses for growth and expansion, thus creating new jobs and aiding to increase productivity of individual companies.

As a result, the average age of United States industrial plant and equipment has advanced faster than in other countries. Figure 1.2 shows the steady aging of United States capital

FIGURE **1.2.**

Average Age of Plant and Equipment in the United States.

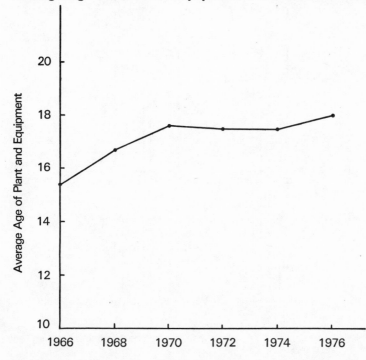

Source: American Productivity Center, Productivity Perspectives, 1979.

goods to a current 17–18 years old. For comparison, Figure 1.3 shows how we fare against our major international competitors. The National Machine Tool Builders Association estimates that the United States has the smallest crop of machine tools under 10 years of age, and the most over 20 years of age. Some critics would argue that this was a result of post-World War II téchnological and financial aid. Undoubtedly they are right. The technology aid did come from us. But as the information in Figure 1.3 indicates, our competition maintained and updated that benefit better. And that was done by outspending us, as shown in Figure 1.4. Spending on equipment and plants is proportional to productivity advances. Most of us know which country has the highest productivity growth and which has the lowest—Japan and the United States, respectively. And Japan outspends us on capital as a percent of GNP by more than 2 to 1.

FIGURE 1.3.

International Comparison of Machine-Tool Ages.

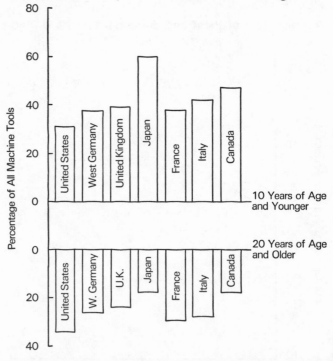

Source: Based on data reported by the National Machine Tool Builders Association.

FIGURE 1.4.

Capital Investment and Productivity Improvement are Linked.

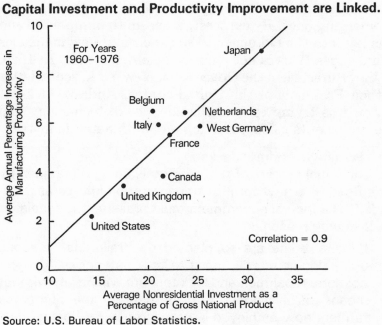

Source: U.S. Bureau of Labor Statistics.

The effect of capital investment on even lower levels than international is quite impressive as the following table shows:

United States Business Sector	Capital Invested Per Worker	1968–1978 Productivity Improvement
Agriculture	$35,000	185%
Manufacturing	$25,000	90%
Office	$ 2,000	4%

This imbalanced distribution will have an even greater effect as the rapid growth in white-collar and knowledge-worker jobs continues. A 1979 survey by the Society of Manufacturing Engineers indicated that by the mid-1990s Japan and the United Kingdom will be even or ahead of the United States in the application of computers to a wide range of jobs like designing, engineering drawing, robotics, and manufacturing. One of the main reasons is the level of investment in computer main frames as a precent of Gross National Product—U.S., 2.4%; U.K., 2.4%; Japan, 1.5%.

Observations of the Japanese government indicate a lack of desire to support mature or dying industries. Its interests are in new or emerging ones. By contrast, we seem to pump more and more money into the old ones at the expense of new industries and technologies. This is not a new problem, however. In 1829, Martin Van Buren, then the Governor of New York, sent a letter to the then President of the United States, Andrew Jackson. Van Buren was trying to stall the advance of technology and sacrifice its benefits to save a dying and antiquated industry.

To: President Andrew Jackson

The canal system of this country is being threatened by the spread of a new form of transportation known as "railroads." The federal government must preserve the canals for the following reasons:

1. If canal boats are supplanted by "railroads," serious unemployment will result. Captains, cooks, drivers, hostlers, repairmen and lock tenders will be left without means of livelihood, not to mention the numerous farmers now employed in growing hay for horses.

2. Boat builders would suffer and towline, whip and harness makers would be left destitute.

3. Canal boats are absolutely essential to the defense of the United States. In the event of the expected trouble with England, the Erie Canal will be the only means by which we could ever move the supplies so vital to waging modern war.

For the above mentioned reasons, the government should create an Interstate Commerce Commission to protect the American people from the evils of "railroads" and to preserve the canals for posterity.

As you may well know, Mr. President, "railroad" carriages are pulled at the enormous speed of fifteen miles per hour by "engines" which, in addition to endangering life and limb of passengers, roar and snort their way through the countryside, setting fire to crops, scaring livestock and frightening women and children. The Almighty certainly never intended that people should travel at such breakneck speed.

Signed,

Martin Van Buren,

Governor, State of New York*

---

*As quoted in *Dunn's Review,* July 1980, p. 37.

Technological Innovation

There is mounting evidence that the highest gains in productivity, employment, and price stability occur in those industries with the highest research and development commitment, the third factor on our list of causes of declining productivity. Industries related to medicine, electronics, synthetic fibers, and telecommunications are among those that have experienced substantial benefits from their R&D efforts.

Research and development not only creates new materials, processes, and products, but it also creates whole new industries. In 1929, Herbert Hoover appointed a blue-ribbon commission to plot the United States' course through 1952. After a great deal of study and planning, the 500 researchers produced thirteen volumes of data. A 1600-page summary did not contain one word about atomic energy, jet propulsion, antibiotics, or transistors. The reasons? Research and development hadn't created them yet. Since 1900 R&D has given us innovative concepts, whole new industries employing millions and adding immeasurably to the national economy. Consider the following innovations and their effect on our lives and standard of living:

1903—Flight

1906—Vacuum Tube

1927—Television

1930—Liquid-fueled Rockets

1936—Radar

1942—Jet Engines

1945—Nuclear Energy

1949—Transistors

1953—Structure of DNA

1954—Polio Vaccine

1973—CAT Scanner

The list can go on and on. The important point is that the R&D expenditures of private business, government, and academia were responsible for these contributions to mankind.

Figure 1.5 shows that the total research and development expenditures, as a percent of Gross National Product, have

FIGURE 1.5.

Research and Development Expenditures as a Percent of Gross National Product Between 1953 and 1977.

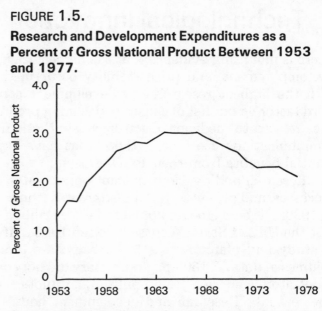

Source: American Productivity Center, Productivity Perspectives, 1980.

fallen from a high of 3.0% in the mid-1950s to a current level of approximately 2%. Since 1967, total cash outlays for R&D in constant 1972 dollars have declined about 4.1%. The government's share of total expenditures has decreased by more than 30%. At the same time, nongovernment expenditures have held steady but have been redirected. The new direction that much of the R&D funding has taken is toward reactive or defensive research.

Facing with limited funds and governmental regulations, many companies have been forced to spend inordinate amounts of money in R&D projects that do not help the productivity situation. A major specialty steel producer estimates that its defensive research is growing at an annual rate of 10% or more. R&D dollars, therefore, are being devoted to staying out of trouble instead of getting into new products. This is a tremendous drain on capital, without adding anything to productivity.

James Abegglen, Vice President of the Boston Consulting Group, points out that in 1966, 20% of all U.S. patents were issued to foreign countries. In 1976 this rose to 30% with Japan capturing 25% of those. By comparison, Japan received 8% of the total in 1966.* A major supplier of chemical, agricultural,

---

Personnel and Productivity Conference, The Pentacle Group, San Francisco, CA, October 27, 1980.

and pharmaceutical products estimates its defensive research effort at 15% and 25% of its total agricultural and pharmaceutical research budgets, respectively.

In August, 1981, *Inc.* Magazine reported on the relationship between R&D expectations and sales increases for 52 of its "1981 *Inc.* 200" companies. The results shown in Figure 1.6 clearly demonstrate the value of R&D. The report found that three companies with R&D investments of 10% to 12% of sales posted sales gains as high as 119% in the subsequent period. Somewhat less was gained by companies with investments in the 3% to 5% range—an average of 53%.*

It seems that future industrial increases in R&D funding will depend largely on the expansion of available capital, a return of government activity to the mid-1960s levels, management concern for long-term growth as an adjunct to short-term profitability, and a rollback of the cost of capital. All of these play a role in advancing R&D activities and, in turn, productivity.

Energy Concerns

The fourth element on the list is energy. We are constantly reminded of the impact of energy costs each time we pull up to a gas pump or open our utility or heating bills. But the impact

FIGURE **1.6.**

Research and Development Expenditures are Linked to Sales Growth.

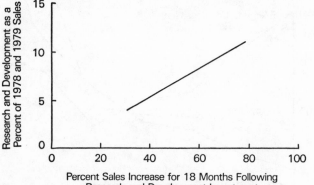

Source: Reprinted with the permission of *Inc.* Magazine, August 1981. Copyright © 1981 by Inc. Publishing Company, 38 Commercial Wharf, Boston, MA 02110.

---

*Inc. Magazine, August 1981, p. 44.

energy has on productivity may not be so obvious. Mathematically, energy is in the denominator of the output/input relationship. Therefore, as energy costs rise, the ratio becomes smaller. As the cost and availability of energy become more restrictive, processes will slow or stop, thus dictating the closing of plants and businesses. Such was the case in the snowbelt states during the winter of 1976.

There is also the potential of realigning our historical emphasis on the substitution of energy for manual labor. There is a theoretical crossover point where energy price rises may exceed labor price increases. When this point is reached, it would be more economical to replace energy with manual labor. The ratio of energy cost increases to labor cost increases continued to decline during the 20-year period ending in 1967, as shown in Figure 1.7. Subsequently, the trend began to reverse. If the energy/compensation relationship continues at the current

FIGURE 1.7.

Comparison of Energy and Compensation Cost Indexes from 1950 to 1978.

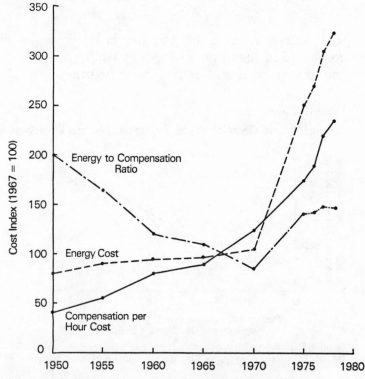

Source: U.S. Bureau of Labor Statistics, Department of Commerce.

rates, the energy-cost index will be 322% higher than the labor-cost index by the year 2000. This condition predates World War II.

The non-OPEC part of our energy problems rests in the balance we try to strike between energy use and the environment. Our often overzealous attempts to correct past ills can frequently overload the balance in one direction or another. This was best described in a letter to the *New York Times* of August 29, 1979: "... that Con Ed's reversion to coal combustion be conditioned on the company's analysis of potential climatological impacts due to carbon dioxide emissions ... is a bit like compelling would-be parents to file a world-wide population impact statement before starting a family."

The changes and adjustments we need to make in the use and generation of energy must be accomplished with proper deliberation, not emotionalism. William Lee, President of Duke Power, at the 1979 Joint Power Generation Conference, proposed that: "To build no more nuclear plants and shut down the ones we have, relying instead on decentralized solar energy and other renewable sources would be analogous to inciting a mob to burn down all bridges today with the promise that by tomorrow we can learn to walk on water."

Human Resources

Some of us can recall the stories of our parents or grandparents about the Great Depression and the hardships associated with immigration to this country. It was during that pre-World War II period that work was synonymous with survival. If one didn't work, there was no food to purchase, no clothing to buy, and little shelter to obtain. That generation prayed for health—if the breadwinner was healthy, he or she could work and obtain the money needed for the necessities of life.

Today, in a period about to enter a new millenium, the value systems of that earlier period do not apply any longer. If we are willing to look around with our eyes open, we will recognize that human resources have been changing faster than our management styles have. Many managers today still use techniques developed at the turn of the century. Some may claim that the real problem is a lessening of the work ethic—but is it really that or a shift in the purposes of work that has had the influence? If the work ethic is defined as a willingness to achieve, then it is not dead. Some of us just don't agree with the purposes.

If this perspective is acceptable, then it is only necessary to look at what people are out to achieve today as opposed to previous periods. This relatively small change in perspective can help provide an understanding that enables management to work with these changes. It is fruitless to try and return to what was. Energies are better spent at trying to mold what should and could be. Consider some of the following shifts observed in the workforce over the last three or four decades.

- The basic educational level of the average worker has advanced substantially. The result is that over 30% of workers are overeducated for the jobs that they are performing. The jobs haven't changed as much as the people have.

- Personal-skill developments have increased to the point where estimates indicate that 36% of the workforce is skill underutilized.

- At the turn of the century, the workforce consisted primarily of blue-collar jobs. Today, over 50% of the workforce is in jobs that are classified as white collar: engineering, finance, secretarial, sales, programming, customer service, personnel, supervision, etc.

- According to some estimates, the distribution of the workforce in 1990 will be mostly (approximately 80%) in service-related jobs. Of the rest, about 18% will be in manufacturing jobs and the remaining 2% will be in farming.

- Perhaps as an outgrowth of challenges of the Vietnam era, or the actions of the government's environmental and worker-protection actions, or the corporate complacency brought about by the economic growth after World War II, workers are placing ever-greater demands on corporate social consciousness.

- Whatever the basis of motivation, management is being pressed by greater demands to involve all employees in decisions that affect them and their jobs. The frequent belief that the hourly employee doesn't have as much invested in the company as the manager is grossly mistaken. Hourly employees have an equivalent interest and a strong desire to contribute to the success of the organization if only given the opportunity and structure to do so.

- While workers are more open-minded toward business realities, they are also more outspoken about abuses and excesses. This creates difficulties with classical management styles based on top-down only communications.

- Technology is advancing at a tremendous rate—witness the spread of computers, microprocessors, and robotics. These, coupled with a greater demand by the consumer for higher reliability and service, make the role of knowledge workers (engineers, analysts, salespersons, customer service personnel, purchasing agents, etc.) more and more vital to the future growth of a company.

These changes have been putting a great deal of pressure on today's managers and entrepreneurs. Fifty years ago, workers were motivated by external forces—depression, war, and basic survival. There were very few, if any, social programs. Today, we need to manage for motivation of the worker rather than for short-term financial gains. How often have we taken actions to make the current period look good at the expense of the long haul? Perhaps managers are not concerned with the long haul because they don't intend to be in their jobs when the "haul" arrives. I sometimes wonder what would be done differently if managers knew that they would be recycled back to the "old jobs" after a couple of years. Knowing that you have to live with the results of your decisions for a long time might very well change that decision. The same philosophy applies to the way we have been dealing with human resources in this country. However, in this case, the long haul goes back about 200 years. Ted Mills, Director of the American Center for Quality of Worklife, points out:

> Most of us either forget or never stop to think that the models upon which most modern industrial organizations are based were created and developed over 200 years ago. The father knows best authoritarian values of 200 years ago . . . still dominate most industrial and even service organizations and the unions they bargain with, even though society outside the plant gate has radically changed its values, and—much more importantly—its expectations.*

---

*Ted Mills, "Quality of Work Life," Address to Centre International de Recherches Et D'Etudes en Management, Montreal, Canada, June 8, 1978.

In order to most effectively tap this new workforce, managers need new organizational models to copy. Donald Mankin, in his book *Toward a Post-Industrial Psychology*, asks managers to understand that:

> In place of its traditional bureaucratic model, there will be increased emphasis on participation of employees in organizational decisions, more tolerance for diversity, a greater use of problem solving groups in place of formerly differentiated departments and divisions, an increased need for interpersonal effectiveness, and a continuing commitment to experimentation and organizational change.*

With the threat that foreign competition places on jobs, organized labor is becoming more openly concerned with productivity and the changing nature of its membership. For too long a time, labor was trying to divide the pie and forgot that it had a role in baking it. As far back as 1941, the temporary National Economic Committee pointed out that:

> When concentration on the production of wealth is abandoned for a fight over the division of wealth, then devices of a low order of cunning are likely to be more effective than the high order of intelligence.†

Business Week claims that productivity is our biggest undeveloped resource and that our untapped potential for increasing productivity is the best hope for dealing with inflation and world-wide competition.‡

How can we as managers and owners of businesses tap into this human potential? Where can we look first, and what are the benefits to be realized along with the problems and pitfalls? How can one begin a productivity-improvement effort—even better, how can one change the environment of an organization so that productivity improvement is a normal way of doing things? Unless anyone be misled, productivity improvement and change are not to be taken as a program. Programs don't have the staying power to help us compete with foreign manufacturers. Programs

---

*Donald Mankin, *Toward a Post-Industrial Psychology*, New York, John Wiley, 1978.

†TNEC Monograph No. 18, Washington, 1941, p. 47.

‡"America's Restructured Economy," *Business Week*, Special Issue, June 1981, pp. 55–100.

tend to have a beginning, a middle, and an end. If we don't improve our collective productivity, the end may be exactly what we get. A jumbled pile of material cannot be called a cathedral anymore than an uncoordinated collection of programs and projects can be called a productivity strategy. Just as the cathedral's building materials will begin to disappear if left unattended, so will the benefits of isolated cost-improvement programs become lost. Productivity-improvement strategies, like the cathedral, are built one brick at a time, with each in their proper place according to a well-conceived plan.

CHAPTER

"On Measurement of Productivity"

Faced with the impossibility of exact answers to questions that we would dearly like to answer, we have three options:

We can forget about it.

We can willfully force the answers and try to use our authority to make them stick.

Or we can devise an acceptable and believable process for generating answers even if the answers themselves are known to be imperfect.*

—Daniel H. Gray

*Source: *Productivity Measurement: An Executive Overview,* (Houston, TX: American Productivity Center, 1979), p. 22.

# CHAPTER 2

Productivity Measurement Is for Everyone

Productivity measurement is difficult to put your arms around. It has different meanings to each business person. It can be a dull and boring subject, but like a person of the opposite sex, once you get close to it, there are advantages that go beyond the first surface impressions. And, like people, measures have personalities that range from the complex to the simple. In many cases, the interpretation and usefulness will run in the opposite direction—simple to complex. There are middle of the road measures that borrow from the positive characteristics of each of the extremes. A question that should arise is, "What exactly is productivity?" If this question can be answered, the basis for determining productivity measures will be at hand. Therefore, the following definition is offered.

> Productivity is a process whereby an organization effectively and efficiently converts its resources into the products and services it offers for sale.

So much for the definition. The next step is to identify and clarify the resources (products or services) and to define "effective" and "efficient." Products and services are those that the organization produces in order to generate revenue that, hopefully, provides profits. The resources can be classified into four major categories: labor, capital, energy, and materials. Energy, due to its costs, is deserving of its own category. All of these categories are listed in Tables 2.1, 2.2, 2.3, and 2.4 with their corresponding subgroups. The classifications are not inflexible or intended to be all inclusive. Obviously, some titles or classifications may fall in different areas depending on the particular business. What is direct labor to one can be indirect labor to another and overhead to a third. It is important at this point to note that direct labor is defined as "any job that alters the product or service in any way or that can substantially affect the quality of the product." This includes printing, cutting, joining, preparing, and in some cases, the delivery of the product or service. For example, a machinist obviously alters the final product as does a carpenter in construction. The same applies to waiters, bank tellers, and doctors.

Indirect people are classified as those that supply support services to the direct personnel—dishwashers, keypunchers, check processors, quality inspectors. And finally, as shown in Table 2.1, the remaining labor categories contain all the other job classifications. The complex makeup of the term "labor" can be seen in Table 2.1. It is more than just direct workers. It accumulates a broad collection of individuals that in one industry might be considered overhead while in another, direct labor. For example, to a contractor, carpenters, plumbers, and electricians are direct labor—they alter the product in some way. On the other hand, the manufacturer might consider these occupations as indirect labor since they are frequently found in their maintenance function. Waitresses and waiters are direct

TABLE 2.1.
Labor Classifications.

CLASSIFICATION	MANUFACTURING	HOSPITAL	RESTAURANT	BUILDING CONTRACTOR	BANKING	HOTEL
Product/Service	Electrical Components	Health Care	Food	Construction Projects	Use of Funds	Room Rental
Direct Labor	Machine Operator	Nurse	Waitress	Carpenter	Teller	Bellhop
	Solderer	Doctor	Busboy	Mason	Loan Officer	House-keeper
	Packer	Pharmacist		Electrician	Check Processor	Cashier
Indirect Labor	Maintenance	Mainte-nance	Dishwasher	Scheduler	Book-keeper	Food Service
	Inspection	Janitorial	Janitorial	Expeditor	Security	Doorman
	Shipping	Aide/ Orderly	Host(ess)	Estimator	Backroom	Mainten-ance
	Material Handler	Admitting	Cashier			Operator
Technical	Designer	Laboratory	Bartender	Architect	Economist	Security
	Drafter	X-Ray	Accountant	Surveyor	Program-mer	Catering
	Programmer	Psychiatry	Chef	Engineer	Auditor	
Administration	Finance	Personnel	Purchasing	Payroll	Adverti-sing	Book-keeper
	Personnel	Training	Bookkeeper	Purchasing	Legal	Payroll
	Marketing	Billing		Personnel	Training	
Management	Foreman	Head Nurse	Maitre d'Hotel	Project Manager	Officers	Bell Captain
	Department Head	Chief of Staff	Owner	Site Manager	Chief Teller	Day Manager
	Officer	Executive Director	Head Waiter	Owner	Check Processing Supervisor	Night Manager

labor to a restaurant, but overhead to an organization that has its own company cafeteria. And finally, one might consider a bookkeeper in a bank as indirect labor while to a contractor or a hotel the function could be considered administrative.

Classifications become simpler when materials, energy, and capital are considered. Materials can be distributed between direct and indirect groupings. Direct materials are those which become a part of, or are intimately associated with, the product or service; for example, the wires used in electronic components, bandages used in hospitals, the dishes in restaurants, nails in construction, deposit slips in a bank, and linens in a hotel. All other materials can be classified as indirect. Table 2.2 shows the kinds of materials that could be included in the direct, indirect, overhead and contract-material categories for different businesses.

Indirect materials are those needed to support the manufacture or production of the products and services but do not

TABLE 2.2.
Material Classifications.

CLASSIFICATION	MANUFACTURING	HOSPITAL	RESTAURANT	BUILDING CONTRACTOR	BANKING	HOTEL
Direct	Wire	Bed Linen	Utensils	Lumber	Office Supplies	Linens
	Transistor Circuit Board	Medicine Bandages	Meat Fruit	Concrete Reinforcement	Forms Deposit Slips	Soap Tissue
	Chemicals	Syringes	Vegetables	Weld Rod	Computer Paper	Towels
	Fasteners	Personal Products	Liquor	Nails		Light Bulbs
	Hand Tools		Condiments	Bricks		
Indirect	Forms	Forms	Tooth Picks	Uniforms	Letter Heads	Paper Forms
	Work Gloves	X-Ray Film	Candles	Letter Heads	Rubber Bands	Staples
	Drills	Sterile Gloves	Uniforms	Small Tools	Coin Wraps	Uniforms
Contract	Maintenance	Food Service	Linen Service	Cranes	Security	Dry Cleaning
	Consultants	Security	Computer Service	Telephone	Telephone	Laundry
	Telephone	Eating Utensils	Telephone	Computer Service	Mainten- ance	Security
	Uniforms			Aerial Photos		Tele- phone
Overhead	Postage Office Supplies	Postage Office Supplies Two-Way Radio	Postage Office Supplies	Postage Office Supplies Two-Way Radio	Postage Office Supplies	Postage Office Supplies

necessarily enter into the product themselves. In some cases, indirect materials are essential to the delivery of services. Shop workers' uniforms, X-ray films in hospitals, and toothpicks in a restaurant are indirect materials. Again, what is direct to one industry may be indirect to another. Overhead materials are those that are needed to support the business in general, such as postage, office supplies, and computer paper.

The last classification included is contract material. In reality this can include labor and/or material. The range of contracts includes cleaning, maintenance, telephones, food service, and consultants. This grouping is important because it can be very influential to the design of a productivity-measurement system. Its importance will vary with the amount of purchased labor or services, and can substantially affect the overall organizational costs and productivity. For example, consider the use of an office maintenance and cleaning service. The question of how clean is clean can have startling answers when viewed from the perspective of cost. Do the floors have to be "clean enough to eat off?" or do the individual waste baskets need a change of plastic liner daily? Cleanliness may be next to godliness, but in some circumstances, only God may be able to afford it. There may be a tendency toward complacency regarding outside contract services because they are frequently looked on as a necessary evil and something done cheaper by an outside contractor. The major advantage of outside contractors is that services can be scheduled when one wants them—after hours, on weekends. Let the contractor worry about the details . . . at a cost to the business of thousands of bottom-line dollars.

The third major category, energy, can be divided into three subgroupings as shown in Table 2.3. Energy is used for heating, lighting, transportation, and in some cases as direct material to produce the firm's products or services. Unless an organization

TABLE 2.3.

Energy Classifications.

CLASSIFICATION	MANUFACTURING	HOSPITAL	RESTAURANT	BUILDING CONTRACTOR	BANKING	HOTEL
Heating	Gas, Oil	Gas, Oil	Gas, Oil	Gas, Oil	Gas, Oil	Gas, Oil
	Electric	Electric	Electric	Electric	Electric	Electric
	Steam	Steam	Steam	Steam	Steam	Steam
	Coal	Coal	Coal	Coal	Coal	Coal
Lighting	Electric	Electric	Electric	Electric	Electric	Electric
Transportation	Gasoline	Gasoline	Gasoline	Gasoline	Gasoline	Gasoline
	Diesel	Diesel	Diesel	Diesel	Diesel	Diesel
	Propane	Propane		Propane		

TABLE 2.4.

Capital Classifications.

CLASSIFICATION	MANUFACTURING	HOSPITAL	RESTAURANT	CONTRACTOR	BANKING	HOTEL
Fixed and Working Capital	Land	Land	Land	Land	Land	Land
	Buildings	Buildings	Buildings	Buildings	Buildings	Buildings
	Production Machinery	Beds	Chairs, Tables	Pick-up Truck	Computer	Office
	Office Machinery	Operating Room	Steam Table	Helicopter	Typewriter	Cleaning
	Cash	Computer	Ovens	Bulldozer	Calculators	Equipment
		Cash	Fixtures	Computer	Coin	Computer
			Cash	Cash	Counter	Airport
					Cash	Vans
						Cash

is located in the southern region, some form of heat will be needed. Lighting will be done with electric energy. Energy used for transportation also has a relatively narrow range of possible fuels—gasoline, diesel, and propane. And finally, some organizations will use energy as part of the generation of products and services, such as utilities and plastic manufacturers. But certainly most companies will have a dependency on some form of energy.

The last of the major input categories to be considered for measurement is capital, shown in Table 2.4. It is simultaneously the simplest to describe, the least complicated to list, and the hardest to include in a productivity-measurement system. The simplicity comes from the ease of classification—fixed assets versus working capital. The hard part is extracting the data in a manner that is meaningful to a productivity measure. Two important questions need to be answered, "What deflators are to be used?" and, "Is book value or replacement value to be used?"

A final point about capital, perhaps the one that gives traditional accountants the most trouble, is the use of fixed capital as an input to the process of converting inputs into outputs. The main reason is that productivity measures imply a "using up" of the capital similar to material usage. This is in conflict with the normal treatment of capital as a fixed "ever-present" asset.

Outputs Are What You Make

The definition used at the start of this chapter dealt with the conversion of resources to salable products or services. The resources—labor, material, energy, and capital—are the inputs that are converted by some process to outputs—the goods and services of the company. The conversion process varies from the combining of highly complex, advanced technology components to create a computer, to the blending of foods to create a gastronomic delight. Of course, should a manager overindulge in either, he or she has the same results—heartburn. Perhaps the presence of a little heartburn is the fate of managers in their efforts to generate products and services. The result of the conversion process is, hopefully, profits—the real purpose for being in business in the first place.

One important relationship must be recognized at this junction. Productivity and profitability are not necessarily synonymous. Productivity and profits do not exist on a one-to-one plane because they are subject to different influences. Effective resource utilization will certainly effect profits—if the market will accept the products and services. You can have high productivity producing "buggy whips" for an absent market, or you can generate high-profit margins by increasing prices rather than productivity. The point is that productivity measurements will let you know how well you are producing the products and services, not whether they are appropriate to the market.

Once products and pricing decisions are made, productivity measures will assess how well the organization is generating those products. In other words, productivity improvement is wholly within the control of an organization's ability to use its resources effectively and efficiently. Profits on the other hand, while certainly influenced by resource utilization, are also significantly effected by market conditions, pricing strategies, competitive innovations, capital availability, and a myriad of other factors. In the measurement illustrations used later in this chapter, it is assumed that the right products, at the right price, and in the right quantity, are being provided to satisfy the market demands.

A Word About Weighting

Products and services are collectively called outputs. And, as with inputs, it would be ideal to use quantities instead of dollars to quantify each of the items. This would eliminate the effects of price increases and other inflationary factors. In some cases a firm has only one product which provides an excellent foundation for measuring productivity in physical terms. A few large and small organizations have essentially single-product outputs:

ELECTRIC UTILITIES: Kilo-watt hours generated

AUTO RENTAL AGENCY: Vehicles rented

AIRLINES: Passengers flown

RESTAURANT: Meals served

SCHOOLS: Students processed

CEMENT CONTRACTOR: Cubic yards poured

MOTEL: Room occupancy

STENOGRAPHIC SERVICES: Pages typed

TELEPHONE ANSWERING SERVICE: Calls handled

But the majority of businesses have multiple products that can be substantially different from one another. For example, consider a few from the above list in a different light:

UTILITIES: Kilo-watt hours—residential vs. commercial vs. industrial

AUTO RENTAL AGENCY: Compacts vs. full size vs. trucks

AIRLINES: Passengers vs. freight

RESTAURANT: Buffet vs. seated customers

STENOGRAPHER: Pages of text vs. pages of tables

Obviously, one cannot simply add different products and services. It is like trying to add the proverbial apples and oranges. Therefore, some way of assigning a level of importance or weight to the different products must be used.

To illustrate the importance of weighting factors consider the following letter you might receive from your offspring at Productivity University.

Febuary 5, 198-

Dear folks,

Thanks a lot for the food packige.
evry thing was ok ecsept for the cookys.
This simester im doing real good. My
avrige is 2.5. I guess that means I
can keap the car. Cause you
promised I could if my averige was
2.5 or higher. These are my grades

Subject	Grade	Value
Gym	A	4
English	D	1
Music	A	4
Math	D	1
History	B	3
Drawing	C	2

$$\frac{15}{6 \text{ subjects}} = 2.5$$

Love, Junior

P.S. My roomy Moose helped me figr this out.

Having been there yourself, you know that not all courses are
created equal. A look at P.U.'s catalog gives you the credit value
of each course. Your recalculation shows the following:

Course	Grade	Grade Value	Credit Value	Grade Points
Physical Education	A	4	1	4
English	D	1	6	6
Music	A	4	1	4
Math	D	1	5	5
History	B	3	2	6
Mechnical Drawing	C	2	2	4
TOTALS			17	29

29 Grade Points/17 Credits = 1.7

You're going to have to take the car from Junior and maybe Junior from the "Moose."

Unless some weighting factors can be found, the sales value of the product is most often used. This accomplishes four things:

1. All products regardless of their importance to the business can be included.

2. Price weighting is a good method of aggregating many different products.

3. Total revenue from operations is readily available from existing accounting data.

4. When appropriately deflated, revenue data is easily assimilated.

Therefore, in order to measure productivity, all that is needed is a weighted ratio of outputs to inputs:

$$\text{Productivity} = \frac{\text{Total Weighted Outputs}}{\text{Total Weighted Inputs}}$$

But this is not sufficient for a productivity-improvement strategy. What is necessary, and missing, is the change in this ratio over time. Those weighted factors and the ratio's trend are precisely why measurement is so complex and so important to an improvement effort. The balance of this chapter is devoted to several measurement techniques that have proven to be successful in various industries. Specific attention is paid to measurement techniques that are applicable to different levels in an organization—the total organization, functional departments, first-line supervisors, knowledge workers, and hourly workers. Standard industrial-engineering approaches to productivity measurement will not be discussed unless they have been uniquely applied or have found use in unusual situations.

As a final note, in productivity measurement consistency is preferred over accuracy. The measurement systems are not intended to satisfy some need for absolute accuracy. Rather, they are designed to treat important data in a uniform way so that the changes over time are reflective of the changes in the way things are done. Although an expression of extremes, the philosophy is appropriate—"It is better to be approximately right than exactly wrong."

Measuring the Entire Organization

Numerous studies and reports have dealt with the productivity measurement of corporate entities and major groups within large corporations. Of these, four have found widest use and will be treated in detail in this chapter:

1. Partial productivity measures

2. Value-added measures

3. Aggregation measures

4. Total productivity measures

As one might expect, each measurement system has substantial advantages and limitations. Therefore, selection between them must be carefully considered with respect to an individual organization's history, data availability, intended use, level of centralization, product mix and homogeneity, factor weights, product life cycles, relative importance of inputs, and so on. Individual businesses may find one approach more palatable than another for one or more reasons. However, each measurement system may be suitable if used properly.

Partial Measures

Partial measures are frequently used when only one or two inputs account for a substantial amount of the cost base—about 40% or more. However, if the outputs cannot be adequately detailed, partial measures may also apply. These measures are usually expressed as a ratio of the total output to a partial input. Some examples of organizations that might use partial productivity measures are as follows:

Organization	Input	Partial Ratio
Municipal Governments	Labor	Fire calls per employee hour
		Road miles maintained per maintenance cost
Weld Wire Manufacturer	Materials	Tons shipped per tons of wire
		Scrap per tons shipped
Trucking Company	Energy	Ton miles per 100 gallons of fuel
		Fuel consumption per maintenance cost
Farming	Capital	Acres harvested per seed cost
		Acres planted per fixed assets

There is no attempt to describe the entire operation with partial measures. The purpose is to get a feel for the one or two important measures that represent both the products and services of the business and the major cost factors.

A college professor once noted, "Figures don't lie, but liars sure as hell can figure." Productivity measures are not immune. From the same set of data one can generate several different conclusions. Weighting factors tend to reduce the "flexibility" available with the numbers and make analysis less prone to gamesmanship. The following table shows a two-year comparison of a hypothetical quality restaurant. For simplicity, let's look at the dinner and luncheon meals served and the dining-room labor force—waiters, waitresses, busboys, wine stewards, etc.

| Output | 1980 | | | 1981 | | |
	Sales	Number of Meals	Average Price	Sales	Number of Meals	Average Price
Dinners	$561,600	46,800	$12.00	$758,700	56,200	$13.50
Luncheons	$198,900	23,400	$ 8.50	$189,900	21,100	$ 9.00
	$760,500	70,200		$948,600	77,300	

Labor Input	Salary	Hours Worked	Rate	Salary	Hours Worked	Rate
Waitresses, etc.	$120,000	24,000	$5.00	$169,000	26,000	$6.50
Busboys, etc.	$ 28,000	8,000	$3.50	$ 31,875	7,500	$4.25
	$148,000	32,000		$200,875	33,500	

There are numerous ways of using this data to evaluate the labor productivity of the restaurant for two successive years. Let's look at five ratios—from the classical to the unique. Each approach will compare 1980 with 1981, and assume that 1980 is a representative year. The five measures we will look at are as follows:

1. Revenue per employee hour worked,

2. Revenue per salary dollar,

3. Actual unit-labor cost vs. standard unit-labor cost,

4. Number of meals served per hour worked,

5. Price-weighted productivity index 1981 vs. 1980.

1. SALES PER EMPLOYEE HOUR WORKED

$$\frac{(\text{Sales/Employee Hour})_{81}}{(\text{Sales/Employee Hour})_{80}} = \frac{948,600/33,500}{760,500/32,000} = 1.191$$

CHANGE = *19.1% Improvement*

2. REVENUE PER SALARY DOLLAR

$$\frac{(\text{Sales/Salary})_{81}}{(\text{Sales/Salary})_{80}} = \frac{948,600/200,875}{760,500/148,000} = 0.919$$

CHANGE = *8.1% Decline*

3. ACTUAL UNIT-LABOR COST VS. STANDARD UNIT-LABOR COST

$$\frac{(\text{Unit-Labor Cost})_{80} - (\text{Unit-Labor Cost})_{81}}{(\text{Unit Labor Cost})_{80}} =$$

$$\frac{(148,000/70,200) - (200,875/77,300)}{(148,000/70,200)} = -0.233$$

CHANGE = *23.3% Decline*

4. NUMBER OF MEALS SERVED PER HOUR WORKED

$$\frac{(\text{Meals Served/Hours Worked})_{81}}{(\text{Meals Served/Hours Worked})_{80}} = \frac{77,300/33,500}{70,200/32,000} = 1.052$$

CHANGE = *5.2% Improvement*

5. PRICE-WEIGHTED PRODUCTIVITY INDEX

$$\frac{(\text{Price Weighted Output/Price Weighted Input})_{81}}{(\text{Price Weighted Output/Price Weighted Input})_{80}} =$$

$$\frac{[(56,200 \times 12) + (21,100 \times 8.50)]/[(26,000 \times 5) + (7,500 \times 3.50)]}{[(46,800 \times 12) + (23,400 \times 8.50)]/[(24,000 \times 5) + (8,000 \times 3.50)]}$$

Productivity Index = 1.063
CHANGE = *6.3% Improvement*

It should be clear from this illustration that, depending on the method used to calculate the labor partial productivity for this restaurant, results can vary from a 19.1% improvement to a 23.8% decline. The reasons for such variations rest on the characteristics of the data. On the output side are changes in the mix between dinners, lunches, and their prices. On the other side, inputs are also showing mix changes in the form of hours worked and labor rates. These variations are not effectively handled by partial measures. All this is further complicated by the following changes between 1980 and 1981.

OUTPUT	Number of Dinners	+20.0%
	Number of Lunches	− 9.8%
	Dinner Price	+12.5%
	Luncheon Price	+ 5.9%
INPUT	Waitress Hours Worked	+ 8.3%
	Busboy Hours Worked	− 6.3%
	Waitress Wage Rate	+30.0%
	Busboy Wage Rate	+21.4%
TOTAL LABOR COST		+35.7%

SALES	From Dinners	+35.1%
	From Luncheons	− 4.5%
TOTAL SALES		+24.7%
OUTPUT MIX CHANGES		
1980	Dinners:Luncheons	2.00:1
1981	Dinners:Luncheons	2.66:1
LABOR INPUT MIX CHANGES		
1980	Waitresses:Busboys	3.00:1
1981	Waitresses:Busboys	3.47:1
PRICE AND LABOR COST CHANGES		
1980	Dinner Price:Lunch Price	1.41:1
1981	Dinner Price:Lunch Price	1.50:1
1980	Waitress Pay:Busboy Pay	1.43:1
1981	Waitress Pay:Busboy Pay	1.53:1

Of all the partial measures used, only the last one, the Weighted Productivity Index, provides a means of eliminating the inflationary effects of price and wage increases. The technique is called "Base Period Price Weighting." By using the costs and prices from the period being used for comparison, in all the other periods, fluctuations in these ratios over time are eliminated. As a result, unlikes can be combined without undue concern for inflation. Which of the partial labor measures are suitable for a particular operation depends on a fit of your needs to the advantages and limitations of each. Tables 2.5 to 2.9 list the primary advantages and limitations of each partial labor-productivity measure.

One final word about the partial measures described in this section. All the illustrations, as well as the advantages and limitations, are applicable to the partial productivity measurement of any other input—materials, capital, and energy. In the following sections of this chapter, will be described techniques that utilize two or more partial measures to more closely determine the total productivity of the firm.

Value-Added Measures

The value-added measurement approach is based on an estimate of the value an organization has added to the materials and labor it *purchases*. Mathematically it is total sales, or revenues, less all

TABLE 2.5.

Characteristics of Partial Labor-Productivity Measures in the Form of Sales Per Employee or Employee Hour Worked.

ADVANTAGES	LIMITATIONS
• Simple to calculate. • Data is readily available. • Easy to understand. • Is an output/input ratio. • Incorporates all outputs weighted by price. • Useful for analysis of competition.	• Inflation effects are not removed. • Does not account for product and labor mix changes. • Assumes the contributions of all labor are equal. • Is difficult to tie improvements to work efforts at lower organizational levels. • Mixes physical and financial data. • Revenue and price are subject to influences beyond the control of most employees. • Cannot aggregate unlike inputs adequately. • Needs a price deflator for revenue. • Cannot be effectively used as an adjunct to financial measures. • May include sales generated by outside contract labor.

TABLE 2.6.

Characteristics of Partial Productivity Measures in the Form of Sales Per Salary Cost.

ADVANTAGES	LIMITATIONS
• Is a partial profitability measure, not a labor-productivity measure. • Is easy to use. • Weighs different labor skills by wage and salary rates. • Incorporates all inputs weighted by price or cost. • Deflates the data if sales and salaries advance at about the same rate.	• Is not a productivity ratio. • Assumes prices and wages change at the same rate. • Makes sales changes dependent on price strategies. • Needs a price deflator to accurately compare different periods. • May include outside contract labor's contribution to sales.

TABLE 2.7.

Characteristics of Partial Labor Productivity in the Form of Standard Cost vs. Actual Cost.

ADVANTAGES	LIMITATIONS
• Common industrial engineering technique.	• Accuracy of standards is questionable.
• Good for incentive-based systems.	• Mixes physical and financial data.
• Easy to determine current actual data.	• Cannot be used for competitive analysis.
• Good measure for manpower planning.	• Output items weighted equally.
• Good cost-control measurement system.	• Does not account for labor inflationary effects.
• Highlights inefficiencies for management attention.	• Costly to update standards regularly.
• Eliminates the effects of outside contract labor.	• Distorted by output changes of the firm.
	• Distorted by labor mix changes.
	• Does not account for capacity utilization.
	• Provides only short-term performance trends.

TABLE 2.8.

Characteristics of Partial Labor Productivity in the Form of Quantity Produced Per Hour Worked.

ADVANTAGES	LIMITATIONS
• Is an output/input productivity measure.	• Assumes all hours are equal.
• Does not mix physical and financial data.	• Does not weigh contribution of different types of labor.
• Is not subject to inflation inaccuracies.	• Does not account for input mix variations.
• Data is easy to compile.	• Does not account for quality differences.
• Results are easy to understand and use by all employees.	• Does not account for labor skill differences.
	• Cannot effectively aggregate unlike outputs and inputs.

TABLE 2.9.

Characteristics of Partial Productivity Measures in the Form of Price-Weighted Output and Price-Weighted Inputs.

ADVANTAGES	LIMITATIONS
• Adjusts for quality differences. • Inflation effects are diminished. • Input and output elements are aggregated by weighting factors. • Easy to compute. • Sensitive to product and input mix changes. • Can be used as an adjunct to financial analysis. • Combines the influence of outside and inside influences.	• Assumes wage-rate advances equal for different skill levels. • Requires extensive detailed data. • Can be misinterpreted due to complexity. • Results are effected by the accuracy of the weighting factors.

purchased goods and services. Thus, value added can be expressed as:

Value Added = Employee Costs + Capital Costs + Pretax Earnings

You will note that this measure incorporates the two major organizational resources—labor and capital—as well as profit. This technique is most suitable for organizations that have outputs that are highly diverse, or have relatively long production cycles. In addition, firms that act as a broker, distributor, or retail outlet for products or services made by others would also find this measurement system useful. Some organizations that could utilize this measurement form include:

- Warehousing and distribution
- Structural steel fabricators
- Book publishing
- Retail outlet sales

Using value added as a productivity measure provides a means of determining the increase in value of goods and services purchased and converted into a business's products. This measurement system adds substantially to a manager's ability to evalute business trends. Compared to the frequently used sales and earnings vs. labor, value added provides more meaningful data. After removing purchases from sales, total labor costs (wages + fringes + benefits) and pretax profit are subtracted to yield the capital factor in the value-added measure.

Sales and cost data for Dig Deep Construction Company are shown in Table 2.10, and Figure 2.1 shows the ratio of sales and pretax earnings to labor costs for the five-year period 1977 to 1981. On the surface, the data are uninspiring—ratios for sales to labor cost and pretax earnings to labor cost are on the decline or going nowhere. However, a plot of the labor cost, capital cost, and pretax earnings—as a percentage of value added—reveals some interesting trends, as shown in Figure 2.2. Labor costs are accounting for an increasing portion of the total value added as are pretax earnings. Capital costs, on the other hand, are playing a lesser role. Several interpretations are possible:

1. Labor costs are increasing faster than labor-productivity improvements can offset the increases.

2. Capital costs are showing increased productivity, thus adding to total earnings.

3. Price increases are responsible for increased pretax earnings, rather than improved capital and labor productivity.

Once managers can determine the reasons for the relationships, they can decide whether or not to add personnel or more equipment, change incentive systems, adjust working capital levels, or even review pricing strategies. The technique can also be used to evaluate the performance of labor and capital. A request for additional people, while simultaneously displaying increased labor to value-added ratios, would warrant closer examination. A measurement control would be: establish manning-level approvals triggered to improved labor to value-added ratios. In this example, a target for personnel additions might be 25%. In addition, average salary increases over 6% might be tied to a labor to value-added ratio of 28%. Similar targets can be established for capital. In this way, pressure can be applied to maximize the utilization of current resources before adding to them further.

Bradley T. Gale, of the Strategic Planning Institute, has used SPI's data base to show that value added per employee can increase substantially with increases in capital investment per

TABLE 2.10.

Dig Deep Construction Company: Five-Year Financial Data and Performance Ratios.

	1977	1978	1979	1980	1981
SALES	$34,900	$40,000	$40,900	$44,200	$46,800
PURCHASED GOODS AND SERVICES					
MATERIALS	$12,500	$19,500	$19,500	$20,300	$20,700
PURCHASED LABOR	6,200	5,800	5,800	6,500	7,400
ENERGY & UTILITIES	200	100	200	100	200
MISCELLANEOUS	3,600	3,200	3,400	3,200	4,200
TOTAL PURCHASES	$22,500	$28,600	$28,900	$30,100	$32,500
LABOR COSTS	$ 3,000	$ 2,800	$ 3,500	$ 4,000	$ 4,700
CAPITAL COSTS	5,600	5,000	4,500	4,900	4,300
TOTAL LABOR & CAPITAL	$ 8,600	$ 7,800	$ 8,000	$ 8,900	$ 9,000
PRETAX EARNINGS	$ 3,800	$ 3,600	$ 4,000	$ 5,200	$ 5,300
TOTAL VALUE ADDED	$12,400	$11,400	$12,000	$14,100	$14,300
PERFORMANCE RATIOS					
SALES/LABOR COST	11.63	14.29	11.69	11.05	9.96
EARNINGS/LABOR COST	1.27	1.29	1.14	1.30	1.13
LABOR COST/VALUE ADDED	24.19	24.56	29.17	28.37	32.87
CAPITAL COST/VALUE ADDED	45.16	43.86	37.50	34.75	30.07
PRETAX EARNINGS/VALUE ADDED	30.65	31.58	33.33	36.88	37.06

FIGURE 2.1.

Dig Deep Construction Company Productivity Measures.

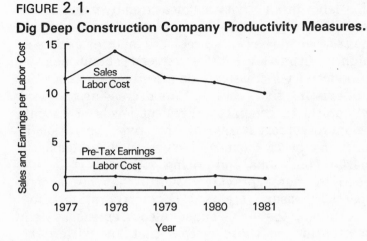

FIGURE 2.2.

Dig Deep Construction Company Components of Value-Added Productivity Measures.

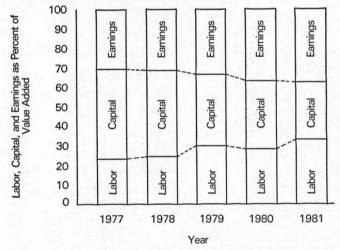

employee. Gale notes, "The level and mix of capital per employee are the most powerful determinants of output per employee. Plant and equipment per employee is the most powerful factor: working capital per employee is the second most powerful."* This is shown in Figure 2.3. The numbers in the boxes are measures of the value added to employee ratio in dollars. What is

*Bradley T. Gale, "How to Establish Productivity Benchmarks," Strategic Planning Institute, Cambridge, MA, January 1980, p. 7.

assumed is that labor productivity, as measured by value added per employee, will increase with additional capital investment. This would be true when the capital replaces labor or assists in generating higher output levels. The converse should also be true. Labor productivity increases could effectively increase the productivity of existing fixed capital, thus decreasing the need for additional capital to generate equivalent levels of output. Which one is more representative of any given operation is dependent on many other business factors, such as capacity utilization, market conditions, and pricing policies.

Value-added measures provide insights that are absent when single partial measures are used. By incorporating labor, capital, and earnings, the value-added measurement system concentrates attention on those factors that are within the control of management to adjust and modify. The advantages and limitations of value-added measures include those listed next.

ADVANTAGES	*LIMITATIONS*
Value-added cost factors are within the control of management.	Subject to pricing policies.
Provides an indication of the balance between labor and capital.	Does not incorporate all the inputs which could have significant effects on profits.
More objective method of comparing operating units than with partial measures alone.	Value added per employee does not account for inflation per employee costs.
Provides a weighted measure of output to limited inputs.	Does not include a major cost of materials or subcontract labor.
Incorporates a measure of profitability with respect to labor and capital.	
Inflation effects can be easily reduced.	
Provides for a more meaningful time-series trend analysis.	

FIGURE 2.3.

Plant and Equipment Per Employee.

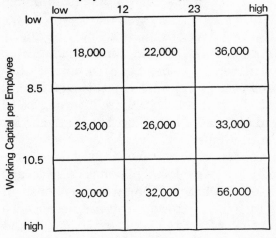

Source: Strategic Planning Institute. Reprinted with permission.

Aggregated Measurement Systems

Aggregated measures are useful for organizations that provide more in the way of service than in products—airlines, hospitals, universities, utilities, banks, insurance companies, and retail outlets. However, this technique should not be totally disregarded by manufacturing companies. Aggregation methods are also useful at department levels, especially knowledge-worker groups. This will be treated in more detail later in this chapter.

Aggregation relies on two factors: 1) a list of ratios keyed to critical areas of the organization, and 2) weighting factors to be used so that the cumulative value of the factors is 1.00. For example, consider the following list of possible ratios and weighting factors for a hospital.

Ratio	Weighting Factor
Accounts Receivable/Total Billing	.15
Supply Price Increases/BLS Index	.05
Total Billing/Total Salary	.10
Bed Occupancy/FTE* Nurses	.30
Bed Occupancy/FTE Doctors	.20
Average Patient Stay/Laboratory Costs	.15
Food Spoilage/No. of Patient Meals	.05
	1.00

*FTE means "Full-Time Equivalent." This consists of all full-time employees plus the total of all part-time employees summed on a prorated basis. For example, one full-time employee plus one of each employee that works 10 hours, 30 hours, and 20 hours, would give an FTE of 2.5 employees.

Each of the multipliers is a weighting factor that represents the relative importance placed on the ratio. The ratios would usually contain the major cost elements in the overall operation of the hospital. The absence of other factors does not in any way demean their importance. Rather, their absence may only be due to the desire to keep the number of factors in a manageable range—usually less than fifteen. Another point to note is that not all of the ratios are in an output/input format. Nevertheless, what is important is that the ratios selected are meaningful to the people being measured and that they reflect the productivity improvements of those individuals.

An excellent example of the application of aggregation techniques to corporate productivity-performance measures is one used by the Boston Edison Company. The system consists of twelve partial measures in five categories. Ten are based on a ratio of a common quantity of output—kilowatt hours—and various inputs. The remaining two ratios are based on output in the form of dollars. In order to minimize inflationary effects, the ratios are structured as financial/financial measures. These ratios and their respective weighting factors are shown in Table 2.11.

The weights were determined by analysis of the major cost elements in the period 1974–1979—labor, fuel, capital, energy, and materials. They were further scrutinized to establish the distribution of various cost influences within each major cost factor. The resultant ratios were selected on the basis of their contribution to the overall cost element. For example, it was determined that KWHr sales to hourly and salaried employees were 90% and 10% respectively. The product of the ratio's contribution weight and cost influence yields the total weighting multiplier. What results is a composite number that can be used by corporate managers to evaluate the performance of the company. Some uses of these performance ratios may include:

- Comparing company performance to individual utilities and the industry as a whole.

- Evaluating middle managers' resource utilization.

- Identifying specific cost factors for closer examination and attention.

- Analyzing long-term cost trends and interdependence of cost elements.

TABLE 2.11.

The Boston Edison Company Corporate Performance Ratios.

COST ELEMENT	RATIO	COST INFLUENCE (%)	CONTRIBUTION FACTOR (%)	TOTAL WEIGHTING MULTIPLIER
LABOR	$\dfrac{\text{KWHr Sales}}{\text{Hourly Hours Worked}}$	11.0	90.0	0.099
	$\dfrac{\text{KWHr Sales}}{\text{No. of Salaried Employees}}$		10.0	0.011
FUEL	$\dfrac{\text{KWHr Generated}}{\text{BTU's of Fuel Consumed}}$	34.0	50.0	0.017
	$\dfrac{\text{KWHr Generated}}{\text{Deflated Cost of Fuel}}$		50.0	0.017
CAPITAL	$\dfrac{\text{KWHr Sales}}{\text{Installed KW}}$	40.0	20.0	0.080
	$\dfrac{\text{KWHr Sales}}{\text{Transmission Line Miles}}$		5.0	0.020
	$\dfrac{\text{KWHr Sales}}{\text{Distribution Line Miles}}$		12.0	0.048
	$\dfrac{\text{KWHr Sales}}{\text{Total KVa Transformer Capacity}}$		8.0	0.032
	$\dfrac{\text{Base Sales Revenue}}{\text{Total Net Utility Plant Cost}}$		55.0	0.220
ENERGY	$\dfrac{\text{KWHr Sales}}{\text{KWHr Used Internally}}$	7.0	10.0	0.007
	$\dfrac{\text{KWHr Sales}}{\text{KWHr Losses}}$		90.0	0.063
MATERI-ALS	$\dfrac{\text{Base Sales Revenue}}{\text{Cost of Materials, Supplies, Etc.}}$	8.0	100.0	0.080
	TOTAL			1.000

Note: KWHr sales include all sales regardless of destination, i.e., other utilities. Generated is Boston Edison only.

Source: Boston Edison Company. Used with permission.

Figures 2.4 to 2.7 show the results of this measurement system for the total organization, capital, fuel, and labor for the period 1974 to 1980. The base line in each graph is equal to the cost-influence factor from Table 2.11. It is obvious from Figure 2.4 that productivity growth, which continued through 1979, experienced some slippage in 1980. To find out why, let's look at the major components of the overall plot—capital, fuel, and labor. Of the three, capital shows continued growth even into 1980. The reason can be attributed to the retirement of a less efficient and aged generating plant. Thus, the ratio of KWHr to a smaller denominator—installed KW—results in a higher performance ratio. The fuel component decline in 1980 is attributed to a long period of inactivity for maintenance of one of the nuclear-powered generating facilities. With the nuclear unit inactive, the increased dependence on fossil fuels increased the overall fuel cost. Therefore, the fuel-productivity factor is lowered. And finally, an impact of the public's conservation of energy results in a decline in labor productivity. This decline does not mean that labor has become less productive, per se. It only shows that if the total use of electric energy drops while labor inputs remain constant, the ratio of energy to labor is reduced. Similar analyses can be conducted for each of the other ratios and measurement components.

FIGURE 2.4.

Boston Edison Company Overall Corporate Performance Ratios.

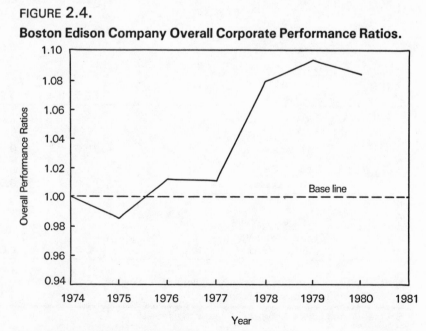

Source: Boston Edison Company. Used with permission.

FIGURE 2.5.

Boston Edison Company Capital Component of Corporate Performance Ratios.

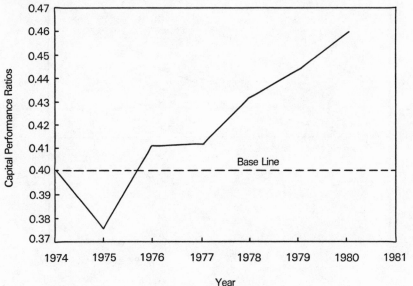

Source: Boston Edison Company. Used with permission.

FIGURE 2.6.

Boston Edison Company Fuel Component of Corporate Performance Ratios.

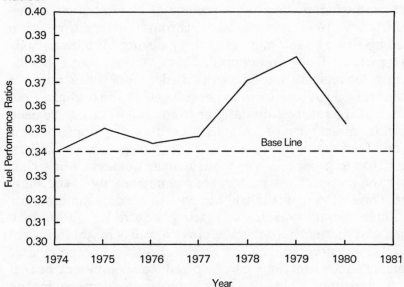

Source: Boston Edison Company. Used with permission.

FIGURE 2.7.

Boston Edison Company Labor Component of Corporate Performance Ratios.

Year

Source: Boston Edison Company. Used with permission.

From this kind of analysis, managers can identify the causes of declining productivity and profitability with more precision than using only financial data or a single partial ratio. In the case of a utility, emphasis might be placed on quicker turnaround time when nuclear units are out of service, greater fuel-use efficiency, reduction of labor through attribution, or a stepped-up drive to sell more electricity during off-peak periods to better utilize labor and capital. In any event, these specific recommendations are based on detailed productivity analysis that can be tied to the efforts of lower levels of the organization.

Each of the ratios, singularly or in combination, can be used by middle managers to establish productivity-improvement goals and techniques in support of overall corporate objectives. Further, other groups can establish measurement ratios that support the corporate ratios but are not necessarily in the same format. These efforts would sight in on specific denominators for reduction or numerators for increasing. Figure 2.8 shows how the legal and production departments of a utility might influence the KWHr's generated; and the engineering, fuel procurement, and maintenance functions can help reduce the amount of fuel (BTU's) consumed. The result is an overall increase in the

FIGURE 2.8.

How Some Departments Can Influence Performance Ratios.

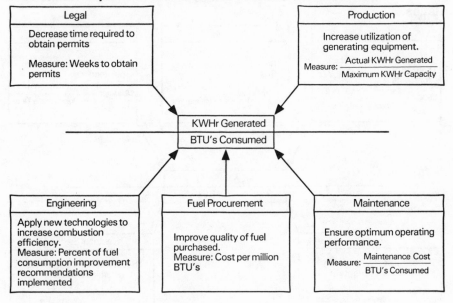

KWHr's generated per BTU consumed. A similar illustration is shown in Figure 2.9. However, here legal and maintenance are shown aiding different sides of the ratio than previously in Figure 2.8. This illustrates how organizations can influence productivity ratios in several ways. Also shown in Figure 2.9 are the planning, security, and electrical systems departments and how they may affect the ratio.

Perhaps the most important benefit of this broad-based productivity-measurement approach is that it can build inter-dependence among the functional managers. The establishment of functional ratios that influence corporate-performance indexes can strengthen, or begin, a team-building environment. The measurement system can reinforce how the various func-tions fit together to support the firm and how, in turn, the firm supports the individual functions.

A second aggregation technique that has found some success is based on a labor partial-productivity measure. Aggre-gation and weighting are accomplished by combining the labor expended on all products and weighting the unit output of the various products or services according to their relative labor con-tent. The result is an equivalent unit of output that can be used to compare different operations or different periods of time.

FIGURE 2.9.

Some Departments Can Assist Differently With Different Performance Ratios.

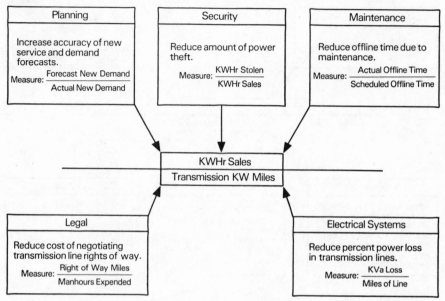

or both. For example, consider a bank that wishes to develop a productivity measure for its various transaction operations—checks, statements, notes, etc. Since the volume for each varies considerably, the problem is how to weight each item's contribution to the labor demand and determine the pattern of productivity. The bank—we shall call it the Super Opportunities Savings Bank or S.O.S. Bank for short—wants to track the following five transactions with the volume ranges shown below:

S.O.S. Bank Annual Transactions

Item	Volume Range (000)
Checks	1,500–2,500
Statements	1,000–1,500
Notes	100–200
Investments	100–300
Collections	500–800

Using a standard approach, comparing actual transactions processed to some predetermined standard, the S.O.S. finds that productivity increased between 1979 and 1980 by 2.3%. The following is a list of the results for the two years.

Item	1979 Volume (000)	1980 Volume (000)
Checks	1884.0	2204.4
Statements	1080.0	1111.2
Notes	150.0	129.6
Investments	195.6	181.2
Collections	716.4	615.6
Total	4026.0	4242.0
Total Hours Worked	184.1	189.6
Productivity (Transactions/Hour)	21.87	22.37
Percentage Improvement	2.3%	

But questions need to be answered. "Is this a real indication of labor productivity?" and "How is labor productivity affected by swings in volume?" In order to answer these, it is necessary to evaluate the influence each item has on the labor demand. To do that, a basis of comparison is needed. Let's assume that 1978 is chosen. The following is the total transactions and labor data for 1978:

Total Transactions	4,320,000
Total Hours Worked	180,000
Average Transactions/Hour	24

From this, we can now compare the output capability for each transaction item against the Average Transactions/Hour. Of course, using this approach recognizes that accuracy may be far from ideal. However, remember that in productivity-measurement systems, consistency is vital—accuracy not so much so. Table 2.12 shows the processing rate of each transaction and the relative labor demand compared to the average transaction rate.

The weighting multiplier is determined by dividing the average equivalent rate by the standard processing capability. Finally, the weighting factors are applied to each transaction volume for the two selected periods to determine the weighted values or equivalent transaction volume. The data and the calculations of equivalent unit productivity for the S.O.S. Bank are shown in Table 2.13. The results are a decline in productivity of 6.1% rather than the 2.3% increase calculated by standard methods. The reason for this difference is the effect of the weighting factors on the labor demand of each item. The result is a decided shift in the influence each item has on the total. This is obvious from a comparison of the unit volumes and equivalent volumes as a percentage of the total.

Item	Unit Volume as Percent of Total	Equivalent Volume as Percent of Total
Checks	46.8	21.8
Statements	26.8	18.8
Notes	3.7	23.2
Investments	4.9	11.3
Collections	17.8	24.9

TABLE 2.12.

S.O.S. Bank Standard Processing Capabilities.

ITEM	PROCESSING UNITS/HOUR	WEIGHTING MULTIPLIER*
Checks	120	0.20
Statements	80	0.30
Notes	9	2.67
Investments	24	1.00
Collections	40	0.60

*The multiplier is determined by dividing the 1978 average transactions/hour (24), by the processing units/hour for each item.

TABLE 2.13.

S.O.S. Bank Annual Banking Transactions.

ITEM	WEIGHTING MULTIPLIER	1979 UNIT VOLUME	1979 VOLUME EQUIVALENT	1980 UNIT VOLUME	1980 VOLUME EQUIVALENT
Checks	0.20	1,884,000	376,800	2,204,400	440,880
Statements	0.30	1,080,000	324,000	1,111,200	333,360
Notes	2.67	150,000	400,500	129,600	346,032
Investments	1.00	195,600	195,600	181,200	181,200
Collections	0.60	716,400	429,840	615,600	369,360
		4,026,000	1,726,740	4,242,000	1,670,832
Total Hours Worked		184,080		189,600	

PRODUCTIVITY CALCULATION

Units per Hour Worked	21.87		22.37

PRODUCTIVITY TREND: 2.3% Improvement

Equivalent Units per Hour Worked		9.38	8.81

PRODUCTIVITY TREND: 6.1% Decline

Without the weighting factors to balance the labor demands, an unrealistic measurement of labor productivity results. The weighting factors transform "notes" from a relatively small role to that of a major user of labor. Similarly, check processing falls from its primary position to a slot slightly below notes. Shifts in the other transaction items can also be seen.

The aggregation technique of productivity measurement offers a major advantage in its ability to account for significant product-mix changes. In addition, the overall effect of substantial changes in resource utilization can also be seen. A list of the advantages and limitations of the aggregation technique would include the following:

ADVANTAGES

Accounts for product mix variations.

Sensitive to changes in resource utilization.

Sensitive to vertical integration of output.

Reduces or eliminates inflation and inventory swings.

Includes the major, if not all, the inputs.

Applies a weighting factor that balances the influence of competing inputs.

LIMITATIONS

The range of products and services needs to be narrow.

Relies heavily on standard costing procedures.

May be used as an oversimplification of cost trends.

Weighting factors require frequent updating.

Total Productivity Measures

Total productivity-measurement systems are both adaptable to most companies and more complex than the other techniques. The complexity hurdle is worth tackling because of the detailed information that can be obtained and the tie between productivity and profitability. The basic principle of productivity measurement is the incorporation of *all* inputs and *all* outputs of the business entity—whether that is the entire corporation, an independent profit center, or other business subunit. As with the other approaches to measurement, it starts with the basic relationship that productivity is a ratio of output to input.

For total productivity, this ratio has to be extended to include all inputs and outputs. Therefore, the ratio is written as:

$$\text{Productivity} = \frac{\text{The total of all goods and services}}{\text{The total of all resources used to generate the goods and services}}$$

This ratio for productivity has a parallel for profitability:

$$\text{Profitability} = \frac{\text{The total revenue of the outputs}}{\text{The total costs of the inputs}}$$

And since revenue and costs are just the result of multiplying quantity (Q) and price (P), or unit costs (C), this equation becomes:

$$\text{Profitability} = \frac{(Q \times P)\text{Product 1} + (Q \times P)\text{Product 2} + (Q \times P)\text{Product 3} + \ldots}{(Q \times P)\text{Input 1} + (Q \times P)\text{Input 2} + (Q \times P)\text{Input 3} + \ldots}$$

This profitability equation can be rewritten slightly:

$$\text{Profitability} = \frac{\text{Total Products Sold}}{\text{Total Inputs Bought}} \times \frac{\text{Average Unit Price}}{\text{Average Unit Cost}}$$

Now back to the productivity equation. Remember that productivity is a quantity to quantity relationship—tons out/tons in, kilowatts out/BTU's in. The quantity portion of the profitability equation is productivity. Now the equation becomes:

$$\text{Profitability} = \text{Productivity} \times \frac{\text{Average Unit Price}}{\text{Average Unit Cost}}$$

The last ratio in the formula is a measure of the degree to which a firm passes on unit-cost increases in the form of unit-price increases. This is called *price recovery*. The final transformation of the profitability equation can now occur:

$$\text{Profitability} = \text{Productivity} \times \text{Price Recovery}$$

This concept was developed by the American Productivity Center, in Houston, Texas, and is the heart of the Center's performance-measurement system. The major advantage to this approach to productivity measurement is that it not only incorporates a profitability ratio but also can determine whether or not profitability increases come from productivity gains or price increases. Which one of these applies can have significant long-range effects on competitiveness as we will see in the example to follow. Furthermore, the system incorporates many of the advantages of the other measurement approaches with few of their limitations (although there are a few limitations peculiar to this system that will be identified later).

Consider a local fast food restaurant called The Fast Food Emporium. It serves hamburgers, cheeseburgers, french fries, and cold soft drinks (the outputs). These are prepared from meat, cheese, potatoes, bulk soft drinks, and ketchup by cooks and counter salespeople (the inputs). The food is prepared on grills, housed in a clean, neat, suitably decorated building on a busy thoroughfare, typical of the many such places all over the country. Table 2.14 shows the inputs and outputs for the Emporium for the last four quarters of 1980. Table 2.15 shows the sales and net operating profit for this same period.

On the surface, this operation looks profitable and secure. In fact, on an initial investment of $50,000, the business is returning 65% before taxes. Of course, some downward adjustment would be made if every cost was included in this example but that would get to be too cumbersome and complex for the demonstrations to follow. The accountants among the readers will have to bear with this simplification for the sake of clarity.

The usual measures of productivity—sales per employee, value added, and so on—also show increases over the four quarters. Using the first quarter as a base period, these measures are shown in Table 2.16. Again, the numbers show substantial improvement over the year—20.6% as measured by sales/labor cost to 35.7% as measured by value added per hour worked. But are these results real? Do the numbers give the true picture of what is happening? If not, then FFE's managers can be lulled into a false sense of security. These questions can be readily answered by employing the total productivity-measurement concept.

Before we go into the details of calculating the total productivity of The Fast Food Emporium, a few words about the assumptions used in this method are warranted.

- Unit prices and unit costs are acceptable weighting and aggregation factors.

- The use of base-period prices in other periods for comparison effectively eliminates inflation.

TABLE 2.14.
Fast Food Emporium—Output vs. Input.

PRODUCTS SOLD	HOW MEASURED	1980 OUTPUT BY QUARTER							
		1st QUARTER		2nd QUARTER		3rd QUARTER		4th QUARTER	
		QUANTITY	PRICE	QUANTITY	PRICE	QUANTITY	PRICE	QUANTITY	PRICE
Hamburgers	each	8,000	$1.25	7,500	1.30	7,600	1.30	7,500	1.50
Cheeseburgers	each	5,000	1.40	6,000	1.55	5,500	1.55	5,700	1.80
Double Burger	each	1,500	2.20	2,500	2.40	2,600	2.40	2,400	2.60
French Fries	lbs.	3,000	3.00	3,500	4.00	3,300	4.00	3,300	5.50
Drinks	gallons	900	8.00	1,000	8.80	1,050	8.80	1,000	9.50

INPUTS PURCHASED	HOW MEASURED	1980 INPUT BY QUARTER							
		1st QUARTER		2nd QUARTER		3rd QUARTER		4th QUARTER	
		QUANTITY	COST	QUANTITY	COST	QUANTITY	COST	QUANTITY	COST
Meat	lbs.	4,300	$7.00	4,625	2.20	5,450	2.25	5,400	2.30
Cheese	slices	5,000	.01	6,000	.02	5,600	.02	5,800	.03
Potatoes	lbs.	3,100	1.50	3,700	1.80	3,500	1.90	3,450	2.00
Drinks	gallons	930	2.15	1,010	2.35	1,150	2.40	1,100	2.45
Ketchup	gallons	50	1.20	80	1.25	110	1.30	100	1.35
Cooks	hours	960	3.20	1,200	3.40	1,200	3.55	1,200	3.75
Counter Sales	hours	1,440	3.00	1,680	3.10	1,500	3.20	1,500	3.20
Energy	KWHrs	30,000	.04	31,000	.062	29,500	.08	29,000	.09

TABLE 2.15.

Fast Food Emporium—1980 Sales and Profits.

	1st QUARTER	2nd QUARTER	3rd QUARTER	4th QUARTER
SALES	$36,500	$47,850	$47,085	$55,400
MATERIAL COSTS	15,360	19,440	21,928	22,324
LABOR COSTS	7,392	9,288	9,060	9,300
ENERGY COSTS	1,200	1,860	2,360	2,610
DEPRECIATION	7,500	8,250	8,250	8,250
TOTAL COSTS	$31,452	$38,838	$41,598	$42,484
NET OPERATING PROFIT	$ 5,048	$ 9,012	$ 5,487	$12,916

TABLE 2.16.

Fast Food Emporium—Other Productivity Measures for 1980.

MEASURE	FIRST QUARTER	SECOND QUARTER	THIRD QUARTER	FOURTH QUARTER	FIRST QUARTER INDEX	SECOND QUARTER INDEX	THIRD QUARTER INDEX	FOURTH QUARTER INDEX
SALES/ EMPLOYEE	7,935	8,700	9,055	10,654	1.000	1.096	1.141	1.343
SALES/ HOUR WORKED	15.21	16.61	17.44	20.52	1.000	1.092	1.147	1.349
SALES/ LABOR COST	4.94	5.15	5.20	5.96	1.000	1.043	1.053	1.206
VALUE ADDED/ LABOR COST	2.70	2.86	2.52	3.28	1.000	1.059	.933	1.215
VALUE ADDED/ EMPLOYEE	4,335	4,827	4,384	5,859	1.000	1.113	1.011	1.352
VALUE ADDED/ HOUR WORKED	8.31	9.22	8.44	11.28	1.000	1.110	1.016	1.357

- The use of base-period quantities to analyze price and cost shifts effectively eliminates the effects of product mix changes.

- Capital can be included in the analysis in the form of depreciation on fixed assets and as profits in a rate of return on total assets (fixed + inventory, accounts receivable, etc.)

To illustrate all this, let's reorganize the data from Table 2.14 into the format: Value = Quantity × Price. These are shown in Table 2.17. The first thing you might notice is that the first

TABLE 2.17.
Fast Food Emporium—Value, Quantity, and Price Relationship for 1980.

OUTPUT	FIRST QUARTER			SECOND QUARTER			THIRD QUARTER			FOURTH QUARTER		
	VALUE	QUANTITY	PRICE	VALUE	QUANTITY	PRICE	VALUE	QUANTITY	PRICE	VALUE	QUANTITY	PRICE
Hamburgers	10,000	8,000	1.25	9,750	7,500	1.30	9,880	7,600	1.30	11,250	7,500	1.50
Cheeseburgers	7,000	5,000	1.40	9,300	6,000	1.55	8,525	5,500	1.55	10,260	5,700	1.80
Double Burgers	3,300	1,500	2.20	6,000	2,500	2.40	6,240	2,600	2.40	6,240	2,400	2.60
French Fries	9,000	3,000	3.00	14,000	3,500	4.00	13,200	3,300	4.00	18,150	3,300	5.50
Drinks	7,200	900	8.00	8,800	1,000	8.80	9,240	1,050	8.80	9,500	1,000	9.50
TOTAL OUTPUTS	36,500			47,850			47,085			55,400		
INPUTS												
Materials												
Meat	8,600	4,300	2.00	10,175	4,625	2.20	12,263	5,450	2.25	12,420	5,400	2.30
Cheese	50	5,000	.01	120	6,000	.02	112	5,600	.02	174	5,800	.03
Potatoes	4,650	3,100	1.50	6,600	3,700	1.80	6,650	3,500	1.90	6,900	3,450	2.00
Drinks	2,000	930	2.15	2,385	1,010	2.35	2,760	1,150	2.40	2,695	1,100	2.45
Ketchup	60	50	1.20	100	80	1.25	143	110	1.30	135	100	1.35
Material Total	15,360			19,440			21,928			22,324		
Labor												
Cooks	3,072	960	3.20	4,080	1,200	3.40	4,260	1,200	3.55	4,500	1,200	3.75
Counter Sales	4,320	1,440	3.00	5,208	1,680	3.10	4,800	1,500	3.20	4,800	1,500	3.20
Labor Total	7,392			9,288			9,060			9,300		
Energy	1,200	30,000	.04	1,860	31,000	.062	2,360	29,500	.08	2,610	29,000	.09
Capital												
Depreciable Assets	7,500	50,000	.15	8,250	55,000	.15	8,250	55,000	.15	8,250	55,000	.15
Total Assets	5,048	55,000	.092	5,520	60,000	.092	5,520	60,000	.092	5,520	60,000	.092
Total Capital	12,548			13,770			13,770			13,770		
TOTAL INPUTS	36,500			44,358			47,118			48,004		
DEVIATION	-0-			3,492			(33)			7,369		

quarter profit of $5,048 from Table 2.15 is set against the total assets in Table 2.17. This is done so that a base-period return rate can be calculated, 9.2%. This rate will be used to calculate the value figure for the total assets in all the subsequent periods. In this way, a comparison to the base-year profitability can be made. Variances in profitability compared to the base year are shown as deviations. For example, Table 2.17 shows that the total assets in the second quarter increased by $5,000 to $60,000. At a return rate of 9.2%, the profit level to generate this return would have to be $5,520. However, actual profits (Table 2.15) for the second quarter were $9,012 (Sales—Materials—Labor—Energy—Depreciation). Thus, the deviation was a positive $3,492. This figure comes from the actual profit of $9,012 less the required return on assets of $5,520. By comparison, the deviations in the third and fourth quarters shown in Table 2.17 were a negative $33 and a positive $7,396, respectively.

From the basic Value = Quantity × Price relationships, we can measure the change from one period to the next by a simple ratio procedure. The change in value is a ratio of the value in the second quarter to that of the first quarter. The change ratios for quantity and price, however, are complicated by weighting to the base year. For example, in order to find the ratio for all products sold, it will be necessary to measure the change in constant dollar terms, or more simply by using the base period (the first quarter) prices and quantities. Therefore, for the outputs, the arithmetic would look like this:

$$\text{Hamburgers} = \frac{Q2 \times P1}{Q1 \times P1} = \frac{7,500 \times 1.25}{8,000 \times 1.25} = 0.938$$

$$\text{Cheeseburgers} = \frac{Q2 \times P1}{Q1 \times P1} = \frac{6,000 \times 1.40}{5,000 \times 1.40} = 1.200$$

In the same way, the ratios for the other output items can be calculated. By doing this for all the outputs, a weighted output-change ratio is obtained, 1.145 for the second quarter. Now, if we wish to find the labor partial-productivity change ratio for the same period, the procedure would be similar:

$$\text{Cooks} = \frac{1.200 \times 3.20}{960 \times 3.20} = 1.250$$

$$\text{Counter Sales} = \frac{1,680 \times 3.00}{1,440 \times 3.00} = 1.167$$

$$\text{Total Labor} = \frac{(1,200 \times 3.20) + (1,680 \times 3.00)}{(960 \times 3.20) + (1,440 \times 3.00)} = \frac{8,880}{7,392} = 1.201$$

The change ratios for all the inputs and outputs have been calculated and are shown in Table 2.18.

Since productivity is output over input, the labor partial productivity would be expressed as follows:

$$\text{Labor Productivity} = \frac{\text{Total Weighted Output}}{\text{Total Weighted Labor Input}} = \frac{1.145}{1.201}$$

Labor Productivity = 0.953

The labor productivity, as well as the other input performance ratios for profitability and price recovery, are shown in Table 2.19. These were calculated from the change ratio shown in Table 2.18.

As mentioned earlier, a major advantage of this technique is the ability to relate productivity to profitability. This is done by using the performance ratios in a *what if* analysis which can be accomplished by comparing the actual costs against the calculated costs if the changes between periods were proportional. Turning to our labor partial again, this is expressed as:

$$\frac{\text{Labor Cost in First Quarter}}{\text{Total Output in First Quarter}} = \frac{\text{Labor Cost in Second Period}}{\text{Total Output in Second Period}}$$

What we wish to know is, what is the value for the second quarter labor cost so that we can compare it to the actual? Substituting some values for the above equation:

$$\frac{7,392}{36,500} = \frac{\text{Labor Cost in Second Period}}{47,850}$$

Second Period Labor Cost = 9,691

But the actual labor cost was $9,288. Therefore, the increase in labor productivity contributed $403 to the positive deviation of $3,492 in the second quarter. Similar calculations for all the inputs for each quarter are shown in Table 2.20.* To interpret the results, one only needs to look at what is occurring over time. For example, although energy costs are climbing steadily and eating into profits, productivity improvements through conservation are helping to eliminate the cost pressures. Even so, full cost recovery is not occurring as evidenced by the negative price

---

*For those readers inclined to check the mathematics, you will find some slight variations. This is caused by rounding effects. In general, errors should be 2% or less. Again, here, as in many of the measurement systems, consistency is favored over absolute accuracy.

TABLE 2.18.
Fast Food Emporium—Change Ratios for 1980.

	FIRST VS. SECOND QUARTER			FIRST VS. THIRD QUARTER			FIRST VS. FOURTH QUARTER		
OUTPUT	VALUE	QUANTITY	PRICE	VALUE	QUANTITY	PRICE	VALUE	QUANTITY	PRICE
Hamburgers	.975	.938	1.040	.988	.950	1.040	1.125	.938	1.094
Cheeseburgers	1.329	1.200	1.107	1.218	1.100	1.107	1.466	1.140	1.286
Double Burgers	1.818	1.667	1.091	1.891	1.733	1.091	1.891	1.600	1.182
French Fries	1.556	1.167	1.333	1.467	1.100	1.333	2.017	1.100	1.833
Drinks	1.222	1.111	1.100	1.283	1.167	1.100	1.319	1.111	1.188
WEIGHTED OUTPUT RATIO	1.311	1.145	1.145	1.290	1.129	1.142	1.518	1.111	1.367
INPUTS									
Materials									
Meat	1.183	1.076	1.100	1.426	1.267	1.125	1.444	1.256	1.150
Cheese	2.400	1.200	2.000	2.240	1.120	2.000	3.480	1.160	3.000
Potatoes	1.432	1.194	1.200	1.430	1.129	1.267	1.484	1.113	1.333
Drinks	1.193	1.086	1.093	1.380	1.236	1.116	1.348	1.183	1.140
Ketchup	1.667	1.600	1.042	2.383	2.200	1.083	2.250	2.000	1.125
Weighted Materials	1.266	1.115	1.135	1.428	1.225	1.166	1.453	1.206	1.206
Labor									
Cooks	1.328	1.250	1.063	1.387	1.250	1.109	1.465	1.250	1.172
Counter Sales	1.206	1.167	1.033	1.111	1.042	1.067	1.111	1.042	1.067
Weighted Labor	1.256	1.201	1.046	1.226	1.128	1.086	1.258	1.128	1.115
Energy	1.550	1.033	1.500	1.967	.983	2.000	2.175	.967	2.250
Capital									
Depreciable Assets	1.100	1.100	1.000	1.100	1.100	1.000	1.100	1.100	1.000
Total Assets	1.094	1.094	1.000	1.094	1.094	1.000	1.094	1.094	1.000
Weighted Capital	1.097	1.097	1.000	1.097	1.097	1.000	1.097	1.097	1.000
WEIGHTED INPUT RATIO	1.215	1.124	1.081	1.291	1.153	1.119	1.315	1.145	1.149

TABLE 2.19.
Fast Food Emporium—Profitability, Productivity, and Price Recovery by Quarter of 1980.

INPUTS	FIRST VS. SECOND QUARTER			FIRST VS. THIRD QUARTER			FIRST VS. FOURTH QUARTER		
	PROFIT-ABILITY	PRODUCTIVITY	PRICE RECOVERY	PROFIT-ABILITY	PRODUCTIVITY	PRICE RECOVERY	PROFIT-ABILITY	PRODUCTIVITY	PRICE RECOVERY
Materials									
Meat	1.108	1.064	1.041	.904	.891	1.015	1.051	.884	1.189
Cheese	.546	.954	.573	.576	1.008	.571	.436	.958	.456
Potatoes	.916	.959	.954	.902	1.000	.902	1.023	.998	1.026
Drinks	1.099	1.054	1.048	.935	.913	1.024	1.126	.939	1.199
Ketchup	.786	.716	1.099	.541	.513	1.055	.675	.556	1.215
Total Materials	1.036	1.027	1.009	.903	.922	.979	1.045	.921	1.133
Labor									
Cooks	.987	.916	1.077	.930	.903	1.030	1.036	.889	1.166
Counter Sales	1.087	.981	1.108	1.161	1.084	1.071	1.366	1.066	1.281
Total Labor	1.044	.953	1.095	1.052	1.001	1.051	1.207	.985	1.226
Energy	.846	1.108	.763	.656	1.149	.571	.698	1.149	.608
Capital									
Depreciable Assets	1.192	1.041	1.145	1.173	1.026	1.142	1.380	1.010	1.367
Total Assets	1.198	1.047	1.145	1.179	1.032	1.142	1.388	1.016	1.367
Total Capital	1.195	1.044	1.145	1.176	1.029	1.142	1.384	1.013	1.367
TOTAL INPUTS	1.079	1.019	1.059	.999	.979	1.021	1.154	.970	1.190

TABLE 2.20.

Fast Food Emporium—Profitability, Productivity, and Price Recovery Effects on Profits for 1980.

INPUTS	FIRST VS. SECOND QUARTER			FIRST VS. THIRD QUARTER			FIRST VS. FOURTH QUARTER		
	PROFITABILITY	PRODUCTIVITY	PRICE RECOVERY	PROFITABILITY	PRODUCTIVITY	PRICE RECOVERY	PROFITABILITY	PRODUCTIVITY	PRICE RECOVERY
Materials									
Meat	1,100	594	506	(1,170)	(1,187)	17	636	(1,247)	1,883
Cheese	(54)	(3)	(51)	(48)	-0-	(48)	(98)	(2)	(96)
Potatoes	(564)	(228)	(336)	(651)	-0-	(651)	158	(9)	167
Drinks	237	118	119	(180)	(214)	34	340	(144)	484
Ketchup	(21)	(27)	6	(66)	(65)	(1)	(44)	(53)	9
Total Materials	698	454	244	(2,119)	(1,475)	(644)	998	(1,459)	2,457
Labor									
Cooks	(53)	(323)	270	(298)	(372)	(74)	163	(427)	590
Counter Sales	456	(95)	551	773	376	397	1,758	298	1,460
Total Labor	403	(414)	817	473	7	466	1,922	(126)	2,048
Energy	(287)	134	(421)	(812)	175	(987)	(788)	173	(961)
Capital									
Depreciable Assets	1,583	388	1,245	1,425	218	1,207	3,135	83	3,052
Total Assets	1,095	257	838	989	177	812	2,140	86	2,054
Total Capital	2,685	602	2,083	2,422	402	2,020	5,283	176	5,107
TOTAL INPUT VALUE	3,504	767	2,737	(37)	(876)	839	7,410	(1,241)	8,651
ACTUAL DEVIATION	3,492			(33)			7,396		

recovery values in each quarter. Similar analysis for the materials, labor, and capital shows the profit contribution over the asset hurdle rate of productivity and price recovery for each input element.

The variations in productivity, price recovery, and profitability can be seen more clearly when presented graphically. Figures 2.10 to 2.14 show these relationships for the combined inputs, and each separately, for the four quarters of 1980. From Figure 2.10 one can conclude that FFE's continued profitability is coming from price increases rather than productivity improvements. In fact, this appears to be the case for all the inputs except energy (see Figure 2.13). The reasons for the energy-performance improvements might result from conservation efforts, better planning of cooking cycles, and improved equipment maintenance.

An interesting anomaly appears in the materials-performance indexes. Theoretically, there should be a one-to-one relationship between the food sold and the food purchased. However, Figure 2.11 shows that productivity continues to decline and that profitability improvement was caused by price increases. A good candidate to a solution for this problem might lie in the scrap rate or the amount of food consumed by the employees. Some fast food chains require that any food not sold within a certain period of time after preparation be removed and discarded. Further investigation might reveal the following data regarding scrap losses and employee consumption:

| Type | Percentage Food Scrapped and Consumed | | | |
	1st Quarter	2nd Quarter	3rd Quarter	4th Quarter
Meat	7.5%	15.6%	19.1%	20.0%
Cheese	—	—	1.8%	1.8%
Potatoes	3.3%	5.7%	6.1%	4.5%
Drinks	3.3%	1.0%	9.5%	10.0%

There may be little one can do to control the bottomless food pits of a teenager besides complete cutoff. However, better analysis of demand and adjustment of the cooking schedule might be a better strategy for reducing scrap losses.

Obviously, if FFE was facing a price-sensitive competitive situation, the long-term health of the business would be questionable at best. This potentially dangerous situation, however, is not revealed by the usual measurement systems. Figure 2.15

FIGURE **2.10.**

Fast Food Emporium Total Performance Indexes.

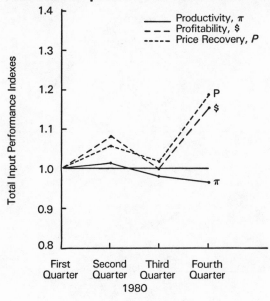

FIGURE **2.11.**

Fast Food Emporium Materials Performance Indexes.

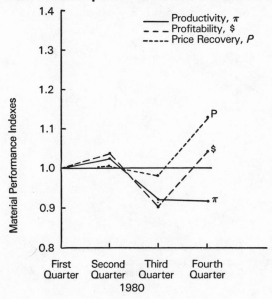

FIGURE 2.12.

Fast Food Emporium Labor Performance Indexes.

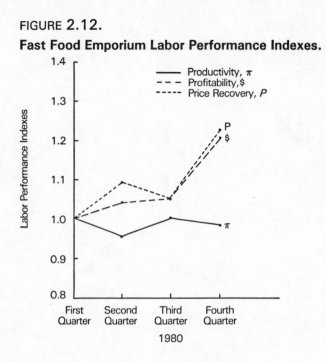

FIGURE 2.13.

Fast Food Emporium Energy Performance Indexes.

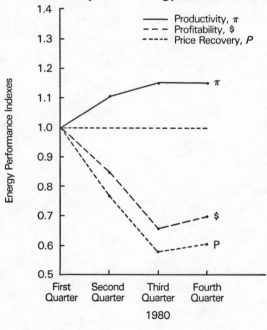

FIGURE 2.14.

Fast Food Emporium Capital Performance Indexes.

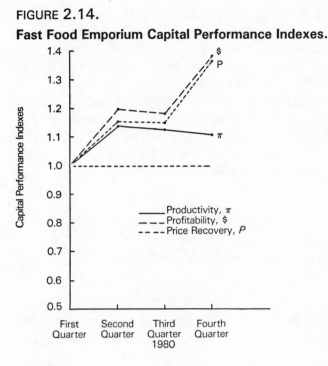

FIGURE 2.15.

Fast Food Emporium Productivity Measurement Comparisons.

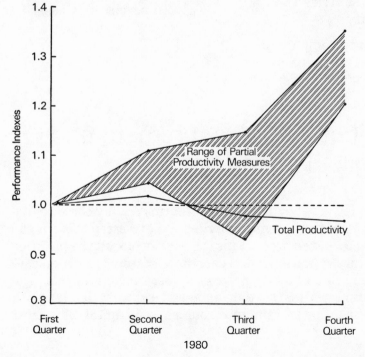

shows the "optimistic" data from Table 2.16 (shaded area) plotted against the more "realistic" situation revealed by the total productivity measurement. Since The Fast Food Emporium's profitability is coming from price increases rather than productivity, is this indicated by the other measures? Figure 2.16 shows the price recovery data plotted over the other measures as was the case in Figure 2.15. It is obvious from this that the other measures are reflecting pricing strategies rather than productivity. As with any other system, advantages and limitations apply here as well. Here are a few of the major ones:

ADVANTAGES

Accounts for all resources

Can be used to evaluate investment tradeoffs between inputs

Accommodates mix and quality variations

Uses partial measures to develop total productivity

Relates productivity to profitability

Can be used to compare different operations or plants

LIMITATIONS

Requires extensive data collection

Interpretation can be difficult

Significance to lower organizational levels may be clouded

Is manufacturing oriented and may be difficult to apply to service businesses

Productivity Measurement and Strategic Planning .

Most strategic plans begin with a long-term (usually three to five years) forecast of the potential market and projected sales of the firm's products and services. From this is developed the resource needs, anticipated margins, and cash flow. Rarely is a productivity measure used as an adjunct to the long-range analysis. The Upjohn Company uses a value-added measure to analyze the long-term utilization of human resources and capital. The IBM

FIGURE 2.16.

Fast Food Emporium Price Recovery Measurement Comparisons.

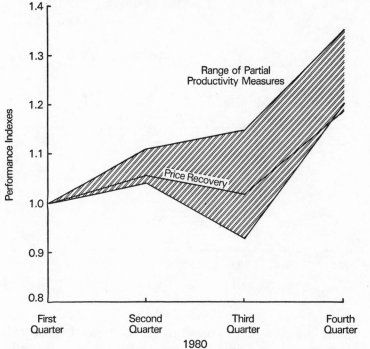

Corporation uses a comparative staffing analysis to forecast indirect labor needs and, as discussed earlier, Boston Edison Company is using an aggregation technique.

A medium-size company in the metal-working industry uses sales per employee and profit per employee in the five-year strategic plan to look at its projected productivity. Not surprisingly, the results show a steady increase for both. In fact, the productivity growth indicated by these two measures averaged 20% and 30% per year. These values directly matched the anticipated growth in net profit. But a total productivity analysis showed something quite different—profits were coming from price recovery rather than productivity. Figure 2.17 shows the productivity and price recovery data plotted along with the company's sales and profit per employee data. If the company takes solace in its data, it may be rudely awakened in the near future.

In a highly competitive, low-margin industry, profit growth generated by cost increase pass-ons rather than productivity advances is asking for trouble. In this case, a smaller company that

FIGURE 2.17.

Profit and Sales per Employee vs. Total Productivity and Price Recovery.

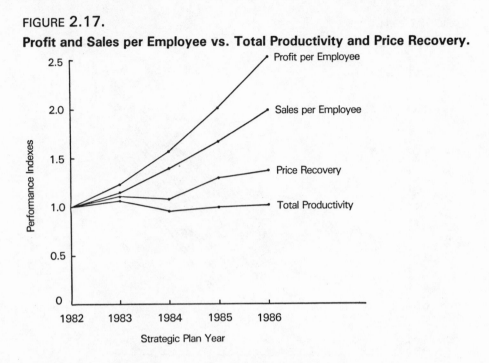

had a comfortable sole-source government contract for aircraft engine components was making enviable profits. However, cruising along for several years on high profits from price strategies created an environment to attract competition. The left graph in Figure 2.18 shows this clearly. If the company had the trends shown in the right graph, it would have been in an obviously better position to fend off competition as well as inflationary cost pressures. Profitability would be coming from productivity advances instead of price hikes. As circumstances developed, the competition won large portions of the business by using productivity-improving technology and more competitive pricing strategies.

Measuring the Department Managers

Many of the techniques described for the total organization are adaptable to the department, plant, or operating unit. The major adjustments that need to be made will be influenced by the data-

FIGURE 2.18.

Productivity Improvements Help Competitiveness.

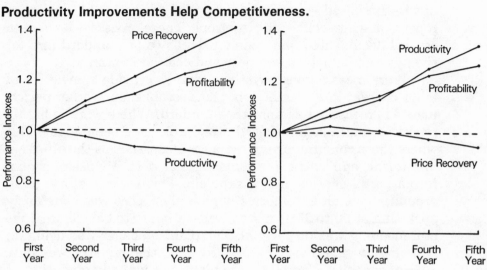

collection systems, the ability to identify and weigh the outputs, and the quantification and allocation of input resources. Not infrequently these decisions will be influenced by the attempt to balance accuracy and consistency. This balancing act is further complicated by the level of the organization, the nature of the work, and the record-keeping systems. And lastly, if an operation is a cost center or a producer of products used only by the company, cost allocations or "equivalent sales value" may not be readily available.

As if these difficulties were not sufficient, department managers' inability to relate to the measure may be the biggest difficulty. In fact it may be a substantial hurdle. The broader and more general the measure tends to be, the less impact the manager may have in improving it. More importantly, however, may be its lack of representativeness to the operations of the group being measured. For example, total productivity measures and many partial aggregations do not adequately reflect changes in data processing. A notable exception will be capital productivity. This is not to say that computers do not increase productivity, only that the actual programming and hardware productivity increases may not show in the measures. In recognition of this, approaches described in this section will emphasize productivity measurements that are sensitive to the activities of the group and are based on data and techniques readily available and implementable by them.

As mentioned earlier, standard measurement systems will not be discussed—especially as applied to routine blue-collar or repetitive white-collar job situations. These processes have been so well documented and widely used as to be standard fare for the average industrial engineer and cost accountant.

Work-measurement systems simply provide a measure of labor content in a specific job. Once established, worker performance is measured against the standard. Where work is highly repetitive and machine-based standards have some value. But where these conditions may not be present, such as the office environment, application is problematic at best. Misuse of the information is another major problem. There was a story going around about an automotive engine plant that was constantly operating at 90 to 95% of standard—a figure to behold until the real meaning was discovered. The plant manager was using an *industry average* for the standard. And the industry was only 70% of capacity. Therefore, the plant was actually operating at 63 to 67% of standard, nothing very exciting. This example also serves to caution organizations against centralized imposition of productivity measures. As productivity measures are applied to lower levels of the organization, there is a tendency to make them highly task specific, such as pages typed per typist, data cards per keypunch operator, castings per shop labor hour, inches of weld per welder. The use of these specific measures does not recognize the complex interaction between effectiveness, efficiency, and quality in many jobs. This is especially true in the many nonrepetitive jobs found in manufacturing and service, jobs ranging from foremen and supervisors to engineers, programmers, and buyers, to security guards, bank tellers, and salespersons.

This section will concentrate on group measures for these nonrepetitive jobs. There are several reasons for this:

1. These jobs are the most difficult to measure due to the delay time between job function and results, and therefore, their receiving the least attention.

2. These jobs frequently influence business activities outside the individual's direct sphere of influence (such as customers).

3. Job performance is dependent on many factors including problem solving ability, assistance of peers, and education and training, to name a few.

4. The performance of the job is not prescribed in detail. Rather, individuals are provided broad latitude in conducting their various functions.

5. Managers and supervisors are better measured by the productivity of their groups than by a single measure for themselves. This encourages and motivates better management techniques.

6. These jobs are less dependent on detailed processes and procedures and more on the encumbent's effectiveness and efficiency.

Measures that reflect these characteristics can be introduced in one of two ways—by imposition from above or by self-development by those being measured. Group-developed measures have been quite successful and will be described in more detail later on. Those measures that are imposed by upper management will be discussed only from a perspective of their uniqueness.

Interrelated Partial Measures

Despite the limitations that partial measures carry, these may be of minor concern when applied to a department of a company. The offsetting advantage is the closer relationship between the partial and the actual work activities at this level. If the variables are interrelated in some way, they can be expressed in a format that demonstrates each variable's contribution to a productivity measurement. Further, if only four variables are used, a convenient graphical technique is available that can tie them together.

To demonstrate, let's look at an order-entry department for The Take Our Own Line Hardware Company. T.O.O.L. receives up to 5,000 orders a year with a sales volume of about $11 million. The personnel who handle this have ranged from 12 to 18 people. The following table shows the data for a three-year period ending in 1980.

Year	Sales	No. of Personnel	No. of Orders
1978	11,100,000	14	3,500
1979	11,400,000	14	4,000
1980	11,200,000	16	4,000

Using the data in the usual way would show several possible productivity measures for T.O.O.L.'s order-entry department.

Years	Change in Sales Per Employee	Sales Per Orders	Orders Per Employee
1978–79	2.7%	–10.1%	14.4%
1978–80	–11.7%	–11.7%	0

Which of these by themselves or in combination are representative is difficult to say. In fact, more complications would be introduced if consideration was given to the average number of line items on each order received. The number of meaningful ratios would then go from three to six. Indeed, when you consider the significance of the number of line items, it should be included. At the very least, line items will affect the time to issue paper work. At the most, it can affect the production planning and scheduling operation.

Let's introduce the number of line items and a graphical method of combining it with the other data. The data for the three years look like this:

Year	Sales	Personnel	Orders	Average Line Items
1978	11,100,000	14	3,500	1.5
1979	11,400,000	14	4,000	2.5
1980	11,200,000	16	4,000	2.5

Figure 2.19 shows these four variables in a format that conveniently relates the data in logical pairs. The result is a productivity index value that can be tracked. The number of orders is paired with purchase volume, and personnel with average line items. This combines variables that have some interdependence. It also increases the sensitivity of the variables to change. The lines connecting the sides correspond to the data from the table above. The circles mark the intersections of the data for each year as shown. From this intersection, the corresponding productivity index can be obtained by drawing a perpendicular line from the circled intersection to the productivity-index scale. For example, in 1978 a line would be drawn between 1.5 lines per order and 14 on the personnel scale. Similarly, a line would be drawn between 3,500 orders and $11,100,000. The intersection of

FIGURE 2.19.

Productivity Measures Using Interrelated Data for an Order-Entry Department.

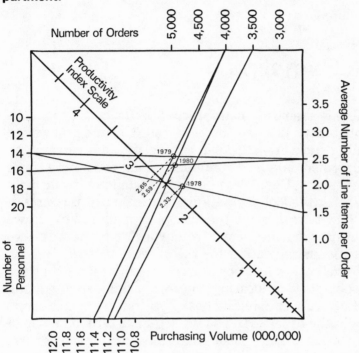

these two lines is circled and marked "1978." The value picked off the productivity index scale is 2.33. The values for the three years and their trend are as follows:

Year	Productivity Index	% Change from 1978
1978	2.33	—
1979	2.65	13.7
1980	2.59	11.2

There are two added benefits of this technique. One is its ability to vary the sensitivity of the index to each factor by selecting the scales, which is analogous to applying a weighting factor. The larger the scale (the more spread out the numbers), the heavier the weight becomes. Small changes in value will yield large shifts in the line positions. The second benefit comes from the graphical format. Changes in personnel levels, sales, order volume, or order complexity can be easily seen and used to evaluate the impact of forecasts and planning data on productivity.

Work Sampling

Work sampling is a measurement process that is based on statistics and probability. It is not as scary as it sounds, however. Work sampling measures the percentage of time certain job tasks are performed, and how confident we are that these times will remain constant. Each of us uses the technique in our daily activities. Why do we look for parking spaces in certain parts of the parking lot at work or at the shopping malls? Why do we take certain routes driving to and from work? Why do we try to stand in specific areas waiting for the subway or bus? In each case we had tried other locations or routes and found that the chance, or probability, of locating a better parking spot, getting a seat on the subway, or avoiding heavy traffic was better in one of them than in the others. And so we began to zero in on one in preference to others. But these conditions are not stagnant. They change with season, weather, and time of day. To be very certain of a choice at any time, we would have to take samples under all these conditions. However, this may prove to be more of an effort than it is worth. As a result, we are not 100% certain that our choice is the best—perhaps only 80% certain. This is a measure of how confident we are that our choice will give us the desired results. As an illustration of the term "confidence level," in a household with young children there is a 100% level of confidence that the cookie jar will have 0% cookies 24 hours after being filled.

The mathematics and statistical principles behind this technique are well documented. Information can be found in any university or well-stocked public library. Therefore, focus will be placed on obtaining and using the data. To do this, let's use a job that is supposedly too difficult or even impossible to measure—nursing. It is frequently pointed out that a nurse's job is in a constant state of flux. Physician demands, patient demands, administrative duties, emergencies, and so on are unpredictable and largely uncontrollable. But if a basic approach is to make the nurse available for patient care as much as possible, we need to look at these barriers to that objective. Nurses who work on a hospital floor get involved in a broad range of activities—administering medications, performing tests, taking samples, keeping records, assisting physicians, scheduling patient services, comforting patients, taking inventory, and others. To identify barriers, it is necessary to establish where to look. Work sampling offers this opportunity. The first thing to do is to get a picture of where most of a nurse's time is being spent.

Many of us have visited patients in a hospital. As we walk from the elevator to the nurse's station and then to the room we are looking for, we notice nurses engaged in several of the activities mentioned above but not necessarily all of them. There may even be occasions when it appears that no nurse is around. If we did this several times a day, every day, for a month, we would have made 90 trips from the elevator to the room. If there were 12 nurses assigned to the floor during the shift and we observed each doing something, we would have made 1,080 observations. Recording what we observed the nurses doing, we might have the following:

Activity	Observations	Percent
Doing Paperwork	270	25
Patient Care	432	40
With Physician Only	108	10
Doing Cleaning, Linens	54	5
Meetings, Talking	162	15
Miscellaneous	32	3
Unaccounted For	22	2
Total	1,080	100

What this indicates is that only 40% of the nurse's time is spent in direct patient contact and care—the activity that directly relates to the quality of health care. Some of the other activities, while perhaps necessary, dilute the nurse-patient contact. What is missing in this analysis are the details related to each activity that determine their necessity. However, one could sight in on one or more of the above to evaluate causes, needs, and possible remedies. For example, if the paperwork could be reduced by work simplification studies, or transferred to aides or done on the night shift, there would be more time for patients during peak hours. Similarly, reductions in meetings may also add to patient-care time. Repeating the sampling procedure after changes are made will enable an administrator or head nurse to evaluate the effect of the changes.

The ultimate benefit of this technique comes from the increase in supervisory skills that it can provide. First-line supervisors trained in this technique can make independent evaluations and take appropriate action at the first levels of the organization. Continuous monitoring of the work group helps to identify potential obstacles before they get out of hand. As a result, decision making gets pushed down the line instead of up. But caution is called for—the organization needs to provide training in problem solving and decision making for this process to work effectively.

Structured Brainstorming

No one knows the job better than the person who does it.
None of us is as smart as all of us.

These two statements are the basis for group-set measures. To capitalize on them, though, an appropriate environment for the group must be established. The process of achieving this has been called by various names—the most common being nominal group technique. In reality, regardless of the name, the process relies heavily on a carefully controlled, highly structured brainstorming procedure, followed by a clarification and subsequent evaluation phase. The results, when conducted properly, are measures of productivity established by the group itself that are more representative of its function than something imposed from above. And it is this self-determination that is fundamental to building the group's commitment to the improvement of the measures.

The process, which is described in detail in Chapter 4, is conducted in a conference room with 8 to 10 participants. A "flip chart" is needed for recording data and information. It is often useful to have an "outsider" run the sessions to provide objectivity and to maintain process discipline. That individual must be thoroughly familiar with the process and capable of handling groups.

The process itself involves seven sequential steps beginning with a clear statement of the session's purpose and ending with the rank ordering of items that best respond to the purpose statement of the session. It takes less than a day to carry out the required number of steps. Consider the following steps for a meeting called to determine the measures of productivity for a department in an organization.

1. Purpose Statement—"What are the measures of productivity that reflect your group's activities with respect to quality, effectiveness, and efficiency?"

2. Individual Analysis—Each participant, independent of the others, prepares a list of measures asked for.

3. Combined Listing—Under the direction of a facilitator, each participant in turn reads one item from his or her list to be posted on the flip chart. No criticism or discussion is permitted at this point.

4. Clarification—Each participant has the opportunity to ask for a clarification of other participant offerings to ensure understanding.

5. Evaluation—Using a prescribed format, each participant selects from the total list a given number of items he or she feels respond best to the purpose statement. These are then collated and rank ordered to determine the group's initial preferences.

6. Discussion—Following the preliminary evaluation process, the list is once more opened for review and clarification before final selection and ranking.

7. Selection and Ranking—This is a most critical step. At this stage, consensus and commitment are generated. The procedure is similar to evaluation but provides several alternative rating procedures depending on the complexity and criticalness of the session's purpose.

As is the case for the other measurement approaches, there is a need for flexibility. The measurement systems discussed are only a starting point. Several iterations may be necessary before everyone feels comfortable with the results. To illustrate, let's look at the application of the brainstorming process to the drafting department of a medium-sized capital-goods manufacturer. Historically, productivity was measured by comparing actual hours to estimated hours. This was subject to gamesmanship because the estimated hours were really an estimate of the time needed to complete the job, not necessarily the original estimate. So another ratio would be needed—original estimate to current estimate. And finally, the cost to correct design deficiencies in the shops were charged back to engineering and made up the other measure. The manager of this department was dissatisfied with these measures for several obvious reasons. Primary among them was the fact that they did not represent the elements that impact productivity, such as engineering changes, experience levels, drawing rework, the type of product, and the long lag time between the activity and the results. To attempt a resolution, a structured brainstorming session was conducted to determine representative measures. Participants included several drafting supervisors, the department manager, and an engineering group manager. The purpose statement was the same as in Step 1 above. It generated 44 measures in Step 3, Combined Listing. The initial evaluation washed out 17 of the original list, leaving 27 for final discussion and selection. The final step selected the following nine measures:

1. $\dfrac{\text{Cost of Drawing Errors}}{\text{Number of Drafters}}$

2.* $\dfrac{\text{Hours Drawing Time}}{\text{Engineering Design Changes}}$

3.* $\dfrac{\text{Total Years Drafting Experience}}{\text{Total Hours of Rework}}$

4. $\dfrac{\text{Total Drawing Rework Hours}}{\text{Total Original Drawing Hours}}$

5.* $\dfrac{\text{Actual Hours per Component}}{\text{Estimated Hours per Component}}$

6. $\dfrac{\text{Component Weighted Hours of Drafting}}{\text{Number of Drawings}}$

7. $\dfrac{\text{Total Drawings}}{\text{Total No. of New Products}}$

8. Index of Drawing Completeness and Clarity

9.* Hours of Research per Overhaul Contract

After collecting data for a year, these 9 were reduced to the 4 marked with an asterisk (*). Results after a year showed the following:

1. Net actual drafting hours (total hours less time spent on rework) were within 10% of the original estimate.

2. Engineering design changes cause up to a 27% increase in total drafting time depending on the product component and the source of the change—engineering or the customer.

3. The productivity of new drafters is about half that of a drafter with over 5 years' experience.

4. The time to research overhaul contracts is about 67% higher than that required on new jobs.

The data are still being collected and analyzed and changes in operations are likely. In the meantime, the information is being used to sharpen engineering estimates, allocate drafting assignments by balancing complexity with experience levels, improve data recovery and extraction procedures, and better evaluate the impact and causes of design changes.

Summary

A productivity-measurement system can add a wealth of information to a manager's decision-making data base. In addition it can be used as a productivity-improvement technique in concert with others. However, if used in a punitive manner, it can cause extreme damage to motivation and can split an organization's teamwork like a wedge splitting a log. This can be avoided by carefully evaluating the motives for the measure and ensuring its use as a positive reinforcer.

In large organizations, total measures may have to be selected and implemented by upper management. In smaller organizations, the closer contact between the various levels of management makes a joint selection of measurement systems advantageous. In either case, success of the system is frequently associated with proper and sufficient training and a clear explanation of its structure, meaning, and use.

The people or group being measured *must* be able to relate to the measure. It must be sensitive to their efforts at productivity improvement and they must be able to make an impact on the measure. Otherwise, the whole system is reduced to a numbers game.

And finally, for anyone who is uncertain about why productivity measures are important or how they can be used, consider the following:

- Profits can come from productivity increases or price increases. One benefits you, the other benefits your competition. Productivity measures help tell which it is.

- Productivity measures the long-term health of a company far better than standard financial ratios. They can help determine if an organization is progressing or moving backwards.

- Productivity measures can integrate financial and operating data in a balanced and meaningful way.

- Productivity measures can analyze the role of capital, labor, machinery, energy, materials, and all the other resources used to generate the products and services of the business.

- Productivity measures allow one to evaluate the investment tradeoffs between competing resources, and the effect they will have on total organizational productivity.

- As an adjunct to financial strategic planning, productivity measures can analyze the impact of various scenarios on organizational productivity. This in turn provides another dimension for development of strategies and action plans.

- Productivity measures can be a productivity-improvement technique in themselves—if properly used. People tend to work at improving the measures used to evaluate their performance. But the measures must be meaningful, representative of the activities, and used to motivate and reinforce achievements.

A Productivity Riddle

What is it? It:

- *Operates on 40 milliwatts of electricity*
- *Is capable of over 10,000 simultaneous firings*
- *Is connected to sensors in such a way that it provides the most sophisticated computer control system in existence*
- *Can print out messages, audibly, in writing or both simultaneously*
- *Knows instantly what information is filed in its memory bank and what information is not*
- *Can be found in every organization at least once*

—Irvin Otis, American Motors Corporation

The answer, of course, is the human brain. An incredibly underused productivity-improvement tool.

---

*Source: Manufacturing Productivity Frontiers, May 1978. Reprinted with permission.

Productivity Improvement Is for Everyone

Measuring productivity is insufficient. A business' task is to improve that measure over time. Just as there are several ways of measuring productivity, so are there many ways of improving it. However, this chapter will concentrate on only one—*employee involvement*—because it is the one approach within the control of every manager and supervisor. It is less expensive than capital investment; it enhances the quality of work life; it recognizes the changing nature of jobs and the work force; and, as one executive noted, "Hell, we've tried everything else."

The last might be more a statement of resignation than support. In any event, it does not diminish the value of employee involvement. However, it does point to one of the major obstacles to employee involvement—management itself. It is well known that managers are appointed on the basis of their technical competence but not necessarily for their "people" skills. All too often management skills are left to develop by on-the-job training. That's why it is not surprising to hear managers favor employee involvement—as long as it happens two levels below them. But we cannot ignore the other side of the problem—the employees themselves. If involvement is as good as it is touted to be, why then is it so difficult to get worker support? Lack of credibility is one reason. Managers have launched so many programs under the guise of productivity improvement or cost reduction that employees have become reluctant to get excited over another one. Just look at zero defects, asset management, MBO, value analysis, cost avoidance, value engineering, quality circles, and many more. The following true story underscores the problem.

The plant manager of a consumer-products division of a large corporation wanted to "get some employee involvement started." A consultant was brought in to talk with several employees and to lay out a strategy. One of the approaches was to conduct mini-seminars for all the division's personnel. The seminars would explain employee involvement and allow personnel to get a feel for it through experiential exercises. The program lasted about 90 minutes with a half-hour more for questions and answers. At the end of one of these sessions, the consultant asked for questions or comments. A 25-year veteran popped up with a statement, "What I think of this whole thing can be said in one word—bohica." Not sure what he said, the consultant asked how to spell it. "B-O-H-I-C-A," came the reply. And when he asked for its meaning, he heard "Bend Over, Here It Comes Again." This employee was saying that he's seen a lot of programs, consultants, and managers come and go, and why should this be different from the others.

So, with suspicion and reluctance on both sides of the street, how can the obstacles be overcome and the benefits realized? To begin, some self-examination is necessary. Figure 3.1 is an Employee-Involvement Readiness Profile that is useful to evaluate your personal readiness. Read each statement and circle the appropriate number that most closely represents your position. After you have done this, add up the circled numbers to get your score. Be honest with yourself and your responses—otherwise the exercise is meaningless. Use the following guidelines to interpret your score.

Score	*Readiness*
15–22	Employee involvement is just not your thing. If you scored this low you might want to look around to see how your attitude may be affecting the organization as a whole. For example, is your employee-relations manager working to minimize relations with the employees? (In one company, all benefits, insurance, hospitilization, vacations, etc. are classified on the budget as *Welfare.*) You may be in for bigger problems than you anticipate. Chapter IV looks into some techniques you might be interested in.
23–37	While this certainly is better, it is still a long way from encouraging. However, look at the individual questions. Are your desires divergent from your actions? To test this, put an *X* over the number that corresponds to where you would *like* your position to be. If most of your *X*'s are to the right of the circled numbers, there's hope. In fact, the greater the dis-

FIGURE 3.1.
Employee Involvement Readiness Profile.

For each of the statements below, circle a number that corresponds to your beliefs about the people that work for you. The higher the number, the more you agree with the statement.

AS A MANAGER, I BELIEVE THAT:

	Strongly Disagree	Disagree	Not Sure	Agree	Strongly Agree

1. Employees work more effectively when they are given the opportunity to perform with minimum supervision. 1--2--3--4--5

2. Most employees will do the right thing at the right time without being told. 1--2--3--4--5

3. Management should provide employees with the opportunity to become involved in decisions that affect their jobs. 1--2--3--4--5

4. Involvement of employees in day-to-day business activities results in improved quality of work life. 1--2--3--4--5

5. Involvement of employees will likely result in greater commitment to the company and its goals. 1--2--3--4--5

6. Employees that are involved in decisions will usually act in the best interests of themselves and the company. 1--2--3--4--5

7. A manager should go out of the way to seek out and use the ideas of employees. 1--2--3--4--5

8. The upward flow of communications is just as important as the downward flow. 1--2--3--4--5

9. Productivity and cost data should be made available to employees. 1--2--3--4--5

10. Productivity and cost data should be used to encourage participation and problem solving instead of discipline. 1--2--3--4--5

11. Involving employees in decisions *does not* mean I abdicate my responsibility to manage the organization. 1--2--3--4--5

12. Employee involvement is important but is not the only answer to my problems. 1--2--3--4--5

13. A manager should seek out employees' concerns, frustrations, and problems. 1--2--3--4--5

14. Employees are experts at their jobs and should be provided the opportunity to improve their jobs. 1--2--3--4--5

15. The primary motivation tool should be recognition, rewards, and participation, not threats and punishment. 1--2--3--4--5

---

tance between *O*'s and *X*'s, the greater the chance for turning things around. Be cautious, though—this is more like turning a battle ship than a rowboat.

38–52   The appropriate phrase is guardedly optimistic. You have enough of a positive disposition to make employee involvement work, provided sufficient resources and preparations are incorporated. The probability of successful implementations here is higher than for the two previous results. Many strong elements are at work to help make involvement successful. You should review the profile and select one or two items with high individual scores and pivot the program on these. For example, if a 4 or 5 was circled for statements 7 and 8, you might begin with small informal meetings to discuss mutual concerns. Attendees could be selected by the employees as area representatives. The first meeting might be devoted to establishing a way of introducing agenda items for the next meeting. Whatever first step is taken, do not forget to include the middle-management ranks.

53-75 In this range, your probability of success is extremely high. In fact, it is likely that you already are doing many of the things to be discussed later in the chapter. Many of the obstacles have probably been identified and involvement techniques customized to the organization.

Even with managers who score high on the profile, implementation can be difficult. The reason is translating desire into actions. Other managers may not be similarly tuned in, or you may be new to the organization and may have inherited a culture counter to involvement. To introduce involvement also implies an understanding of the barriers to be faced.

- Insufficient Resources. This does not imply that all that is needed is to throw money at the problem, although some will be needed. You also need to dedicate some currently available people, space, publications, and the like, to the effort. The key word is *dedicated.*

- Quick Fix Program. Changes do not occur overnight. This is doubly true with employee involvement because you are trying to change decades of neglect. Start small and build on small successes. Do not try to bite off too much the first time.

- Top Management Commitment. Without this, nothing happens. It must go beyond the supportive memo and bulletin notices. Only participation in the training and availability and willingness to participate will do.

- Inappropriate Techniques. The selection of involvement techniques must be carefully thought out. Because your golfing buddy has had success with quality circles is no guarantee of your success. Your organization's culture, history, and immediate and long-range plans should determine the approach to take.

- Fear of Job Loss. This applies to the first-level worker and up. Participative management, although ill founded, presents certain risks and threats in the minds of supervisors and middle managers. They are concerned that their people will solve the problems they have been unable to and will put them in a bad light. First-level employees are concerned that their ideas and improvements may cause job reductions. Two approaches to consider are: 1) guarantee no reductions as a result of involvement, and 2) put this promise in writing. (This, of course, does not preclude reductions due to business downturns.)

- Short-circuit Training. No known participative techniques can be simply and easily plugged into an organization. All require some level of training, which is usually expensive and lengthy. If the involvement is to grow, nourish, and last, beware of the lowest bidder. You can easily short-change yourself by buying an abbreviated, less-expensive package. With training, as everything, you get what you pay for.

- Slow Responsiveness. Nothing will destroy the effort quicker than to be too busy to respond to lower-level ideas, suggestions, or problem solutions. A manager does not have to accept them on face value but he or she does have to listen to them. If feedback comes six months or more after the fact, you discourage further involvement.

- Too Little Involvement Too Late. Get the various levels of the organization involved with the project as soon as *practical*, not as soon as possible. This is an important distinction. What is possible may not be practical, from the employee relations (or union relations) point of view. If relations are good, get employees involved in the planning stages. If the opposite is true, you should present a detailed plan of action with enough flexibility to incorporate new ideas.

- Buying Involvement. There is no hard evidence that a higher degree of employee involvement is associated with financial rewards. Suggestion systems and quality-circle programs have functioned well with and without financial incentives. None, however, survive very long without recognition of the people involved. There are even cases where quality circles operate on a nonpayment basis alongside "paying" suggestion systems. What is surprising is that the ideas worked on in the circles are not submitted to the paying system—a strong statement for the motivating force of peer recognition and the feeling of contributing.

Even if these barriers are overcome, failure can still result. One cause is related to the tendency to latch onto a technique at the exclusion of all others. Remember BOHICA! A second cause is the lack of honesty with the involvement process. Do not use participation to ratify your decisions by involving only those that agree with you. And thirdly, do not ignore the input of the employees. If your staff is unanimous about a course of action or the hiring of a particular individual, listen to the reasons carefully before you decide whether or not to ignore their advice.

With this groundwork complete, it is time to look at several employee-involvement techniques. Based on case studies, we will look at quality circles, incentive systems, and suggestion systems. While we will look at successes, we will also look at failures. As you might imagine, the failures are hard to come by, but those you do discover go a long way in teaching us the real difficulties of employee-involvement programs.

Unions are People, Too

The notion that workers had nothing to lose but their chains was replaced by a recognition that if we didn't live together on the basis of mutual respect we would always stay in chains. I started with saying "Down with the bosses." Now I'm a little smarter. If they go down, our people go down with them. —David Dubinsky*

---

*David Dubinsky and A. H. Raskin, *David Dubinsky: A Life with Labor* (New York: Simon and Schuster, 1977), p. 351.

Any thoughtful manager will recognize the changes that have occurred in the labor movement in the last twenty years. The labor movement has become more responsive to the needs and aspirations of the large number of its younger, more educated members. This has become even more important as unions have focused on organizing white-collar, service industry, and government workers. Another driving force for change has been the steady decline in the number of representation elections won by labor unions. According to the National Labor Relations Board, union wins have declined from 59% of the elections in 1967 to 45% in 1979. As the following table shows, this decline has been steady over this period.

Year	Percent of Elections Won
1967	59.0
1969	54.6
1971	53.2
1973	51.1
1975	48.2
1977	46.0
1979	45.0

And finally, the impact of foreign products in domestic markets has resulted in heavy unemployment in basic industries. This has added more fuel to the fires of change.

While the adversary relationship between union and management is still present, relations have started to take on new dimensions. MOST, PEP, UNION JACK, and TOP NOTCH are acronyms for joint labor-management efforts in the construction industry. National quality-of-work-life agreements have been signed by the United Auto Workers, the United Steel Workers, the International Brotherhood of Electrical Workers, and the Telecommunication International Union. A new environment is forming. But these are either isolated situations or national agreements and do not necessarily apply to local union negotiations.

Every company and every local union has its own style and approach to labor negotiations and relations. There is no industry-wide or company-wide approach. However, the introduction of employee involvement or quality-of-work-life programs must deal with the real concerns and benefits these concepts present to unions (see Table 3.1). From managements' perspective, employee involvement can resolve problems that might attract union organizing drives. (But do not attempt this as an anti-union strategy; it will surely backfire.)

To begin a program in a unionized environment, consider the following points:

- Provide short-term job and salary protection.

- Involve union leadership as early as practical.

- Pursue changes in a logical and carefully planned manner.

- Maintain an ongoing flow of two-way communications.

- Present the program honestly and openly.

- Avoid any infringement of contractual conditions.

- Work toward building mutual respect.

- Remember that how things look is just as important as how things are.

TABLE **3.1.**

Employee Involvement Concerns and Benefits.

UNION CONCERNS
- They fear the undermining of the collective bargaining and grievance processes.
- The effort may chip away at benefits achieved through bargaining.
- Old suspicions die hard and may create obstacles.
- How do they advise membership that demanding less may be better in the long term?

UNION BENEFITS
- Grievances may be easier to settle at the first level.
- Reelection rate of officers that back QWL/EI activities is very high.
- Negotiation environment will be substantially improved.
- With increased productivity and profits, there may be more opportunities to negotiate higher wages and benefits.
- Unions no longer have to prove they can fight, bargain, or strike; they do have to prove they can solve problems.
- QWL/EI support can help to overcome the image of belligerence and aggression held by many unions.

Adapted from Charles G. Buick, "What's in It for the Unions," *Fortune*, August 24, 1981, pp. 88–92

Quality Circles

The quality-circle movement in the United States has been primarily tied to cost reduction, productivity improvement, quality of work life, employee involvement, and decision-making or problem-solving activities. Only rarely has it been implemented for the original Japanese purpose—to improve product and process quality. Anyone who was a consumer or businessperson in the early 1950s will recall that "Made in Japan" was synonymous with junk. A look at the watch on your wrist, the calculator on your desk, the stereo in your family room, your SLR camera, or the car that one in four of you drive, will quickly show the change that has occurred in a few short decades. To say quality circles is the reason would be absurd. However, to say that this process was an outgrowth of Japan's obsession with improving product quality would be more accurate.

The need to change was driven by a combined effort of the government, businesses, and the financial community in order to improve Japan's position on the international marketplace and to avoid economic chaos. Quality products had to be produced. Japan's image had to be changed. No small part of the credit must go to two Americans, Dr. W. Edward Deming and Dr. Joseph Juran, internationally recognized experts in statistical quality-control methodology and management of the quality function. From their lectures and teachings came the foundation of modern Japan's quality consciousness. But the translation of these foundations into a business reality was the role of the Union of Japanese Scientists and Engineers (JUSE). JUSE's vital role was in the diffusion of quality-control practices, its getting first-level supervision involved in quality-control problem solving, and creating a formal structure for these supervisors to share their experiences with others outside their company.*

As the quality problem began to subside, new problems started to come under the examination of Japanese quality-control circles. As Abraham Maslow pointed out, once a need is satisfied, it is no longer a need. In its wake emerges another, new need. So it was the case for quality-control circles. Now they are involved in everything from quality to absenteeism. A distribution of circle activities is listed below.†

---

*Robert E. Cole, *Work, Mobility and Participation: A Comparative Study of America's and Japanese Industry.* University of California Press, Berkeley, 1979.

†Ira B. Gregerman, "Introduction to Quality Circles: An Approach to Participative Problem Solving," *Industrial Management,* Sept.–Oct., 1979, p. 22.

Problem Area	Percentage of Activity
Product or Process Quality	22.4%
Efficiency of Operations	12.0%
Cost Reduction or Effectiveness	11.2%
Equipment Functions or Maintenance	10.4%
Morale, Attitudes, and Climate	9.6%
Process or Operations Control	8.8%
Absenteeism	7.2%
Health and Safety	4.0%
Training	3.2%
Others	11.0%

The lesson to be learned from this is that, once started, participative techniques may lead into areas normally outside the concern of first-level employees. To avoid this, if you are so inclined, groundrules must be established at the beginning of the process.

A Matter of Style

There is little question that the Japanese style of management is different from the American style. So too are the philosophies of operations and quality. While Americans look at quality and costs as opposing forces, the Japanese look at quality as a way of achieving lower costs. One reason is that in Japan operational flexibility and dependability are not viewed as being totally counter to each other as they tend to be viewed here.* This is illustrated in Figure 3.2.

Robert H. Hayes of the Harvard Business School, writing about his trip to Japan, noted several interesting characteristics and results of the Japanese style.†

- Cleanliness is apparent everywhere—in uniforms, machines, and work stations.

- Concern and care for equipment is so high that machines are often left running unattended into unmanned night shifts.

---

*Steven C. Wheelwright, "Japan—Where Operations Really Are Strategic," *Harvard Business Review,* July–August, 1981.

†Robert H. Hayes, "Why Japanese Factories Work," *Harvard Business Review,* July–August, 1981.

FIGURE 3.2.

Japanese and American Views of Quality, Costs, Dependability, and Flexibility.

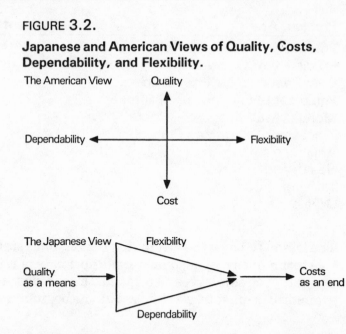

- Problem solving is so broad based that quality defects are measured in tenths of one percent.

- Product quality is the responsibility of the production worker, not the inspector.

- Competition in world markets is based on reliable, defect-free products delivered on time at low cost.

- The company shares its successes with the workers.

Are You Ready for Quality Circles?

The literature is full of articles supporting the benefits of quality circles. Cost/benefit ratios have been reported as high as 1:8. No doubt these are real and it is perhaps because of these reported returns that so many managers have jumped on the bandwagon. Several hundred organizations have several thousand circles functioning. The lessons learned from these efforts—both successful and not—provide some guidelines for you to consider and evaluate.

Management Style. As was discussed earlier, a leaning toward a participative-management approach is necessary for successful employee involvement. If you have difficulty with this or if you scored low on the readiness profile, all is not lost. Specific techniques, such as quality circles, can be structured to provide a buffer between the employees and a top manager who favors the technique but does not want to be involved.

Labor Relations. If a company has a history of good labor-management relations, quality circles have a good chance of getting started and growing. Look at the absentee rate, turnover statistics, grievance procedure (union and nonunion), complaints about benefits' administration, and other data that can indicate the extent of cooperation or lack of it.

First-line and Middle Managers. All too often programs are not successful because middle managers and supervisors were not included in the planning and implementation process. Quality circles, to be successful, must have the support of these managers. First-line supervisors are the circle leaders and their managers are needed for support and to facilitate inter-departmental activities. Middle managers must also be available for presentations by the circle members. These presentations are very important because they are the means by which workers notify management of the results of their problem-solving activities.

Training. It is impossible to implement a quality circle program without extensive training. Two basic approaches are most common: one is an intensive two-day session and the second is the circles' meeting weekly and extending over an eight to ten-week period. Circle leaders and facilitators almost always receive training in intensive 2–5 day workshops. In any event, short circuiting the training will surely blow the fuse on long-term success.

Managing the Program. You will probably have to add at least one person for each group of ten functioning circles. This individual would be the program facilitator. His or her role is to manage the effort and ensure that problems are resolved and that resources are available to the circle as needed. Although you may find someone in house for the role, that person's job would still have to be performed. Until you can afford an extra person, it is unwise to begin. Part-time facilitators will give part-time results.

Circle Leadership. Since the circle is made up of workers from the same area or discipline, the leader is invariably that group's supervisor. This is fine since it avoids split loyalties between job leadership and circle leadership.

Steering Committee. Consisting of representatives from the major functions, the committee provides the direction and guidance for the circle activities. In addition it establishes the areas that are off-limits to the circle—usually wages, grievances, benefits, etc. The steering committee can also serve as a buffer to the nonsupportive management styles mentioned earlier.

Continuity. A problem that has plagued many quality circle efforts is changes in personnel. Leaders are promoted or transferred, leaving a new supervisor the problem of continuing the process. This problem can be minimized by providing leadership training to all supervisors—not just those interested in circles. A parallel problem is the consultative manager who is replaced by an autocrat that does not believe in the concept. Again, the steering committee can help indoctrinate the new manager.

Voluntary Participation. Allowing employees to join on a voluntary basis is almost a necessity in union environments. But it serves another purpose—it allows those workers not really interested to stay out without embarrassment. Supervisors, on the other hand, should all be trained. Starting a circle in their area should be voluntary. Some credit the voluntary concept to Japan, but as one observer of Japanese circles noted, "In Japan it's an employee's honorable duty to volunteer."

Beginning Slowly. After spending several thousands of dollars on materials, training time, and consultant fees, it is difficult for today's manager to wait patiently for a return on that investment. But that is what is necessary. The kiss of death comes from managerial overcontrol and the imposition of costs, savings, and deadline requirements. Some circles may not show savings for a year or more.

Problem Selectivity. An objective of quality circles is to have the circle members solve problems that affect *their* jobs, not management's. So a manager must avoid selecting the problem for them to work on—another difficult thing for some managers. However, if this is not done, it will eventually lead to failure of the program.

Employee Involvement. Participation in quality circle activities is far from unanimous. Organizations that report hundreds of circles represent only 10% of the total eligible employees. In smaller operations the involvement may be only a few percent. If there is a lot of attention paid to a small minority, what is to be done for the substantial majority? This issue will have to be faced as the movement progresses in your organization.

With all of these hurdles, concerns, and pitfalls, why do so many managers opt for quality circles? Certainly there is some amount of bandwagoning, self-interest, and profitability motivation. And just as certainly there are those who do it for altruistic reasons. But the vast majority gets involved for a multiplicity of reasons. These can be collated into nine benefits as described below.*

Awareness	• Increases management's awareness of employee ideas.
	• Increases employee awareness of management's desire for ideas.
	• Increases employee awareness of the need for innovation.
Commitment	• Creates an employee commitment to the organization, its product/service quality, and coworkers.
	• Creates a commitment by the organization to employee ideas.
Communications	• Improves supervisory/employee communications.
	• Facilitates upward communications.

---

*William B. Werther, Jr., "Going in Circles With Quality Circles?" Faculty Working Paper, College of Business Administration, Arizona State University, Tempe, Arizona. Reprinted with permission.

Competitiveness	• Allows the firm to become more competitive through improved costs, quality, and/or commitment to quality of work life.
	• Improves recruiting and retention of quality employees that enhances competitiveness.
Development	• Develops supervisors into better leaders and decision makers by providing them with new tools.
	• Develops employees to think as managers and gives them new decision-making tools.
Innovation	• Encourages innovation through receptivity to employee ideas.
Respect	• Shows management's respect for the needs and ideas of employees.
	• Allows the supervisor to earn the respect of employees.
Satisfaction	• Enhances employee satisfaction through participation in decision making.
	• Enhances supervisory satisfaction by improving communication.
	• Reduces employee and supervisory dissatisfaction caused by resistance to change.
Teamwork	• Requires teamwork for successful quality circle meeting.
	• Furthers teamwork outside the quality circle meetings.

Quality Circle Fundamentals

A quality circle is a small group of employees, usually from the same work area, who meet regularly to identify and solve problems that affect their jobs. Implementation of solutions is also the circle's responsibility.

Through formal training, circle members develop problem-solving skills that are applied to the work environment. There are six major skills: brainstorming, pareto analysis, cause-and-effect diagramming, data gathering, graphics, and presentation techniques.

Brainstorming is similar to the nominal group technique but without the formalized rank ordering and voting procedure. The philosophy is the same with regard to criticism and maximization of input. Pareto analysis is a technique used to separate the trivial many from the vital few. It is similar to the 80–20 rule of thumb commonly used. For example, 80% of inventory value is in 20% of the items in inventory, 80% of sales comes from 20% of the customers, 80% of rushing touchdowns comes from 20% of the running backs.

Cause and effect diagrams are a graphical means of ordering the results of a brainstorming session. Suppose a group's problem was to determine ways of improving human relations. A brainstorming session might yield a list of characteristics such as the following:*

Good workers

High cooperativeness

Sense of responsibility

High motivation

Worker health

Sociability of workers

Constructive competition

Noncomplaining workers

Good supervisors

Supervisor listens to workers

Good instructor

Leadership ability

Just and fair treatment

Supervisor relates to workers

Dedicated to job

Clear policies

Good supervisor-worker relations

Mutual referral of problems

Mutual appreciation

Open discussions

Frankness

Consideration of others' perspectives

Coordinated effort

Good work environment

Good atmosphere

Two-way communications

Teamwork

Safe workplace

Good work atmosphere

Good feeling about job

A pleasant workplace

Equal opportunities

Source: *Japan Quality Control Circles: Quality Control Circle Case Studies,* Asian Productivity Organization, Tokyo, Japan, 1972, p. 17.

To put these items in some pattern or sense of order is the purpose of the cause-and-effect diagram. Figure 3.3. shows how these 32 factors might be grouped. To read the diagram one only needs to follow the arrows in reverse. For example, improved human relations is caused by good workers, good supervisors, supervisor-worker relations, and a pleasant workplace. These in turn are effects that have their own causes. To illustrate, good supervisors are caused by devotion to the job, clear policies, and leadership ability. And once again leadership ability is an effect caused by being a good instructor and listener, being fair and just, and relating to the workers.

This graphical technique places all the brainstormed items in bite-sized pieces grouped into logical categories. The circle then selects likely causes from each category for evaluation. Out of this evaluation comes the most likely cause for final testing and presentation to management as the solution.

Data gathering is used to identify problems and verify possible solutions. Although founded on statistical methods, it has been reduced to simple checklist format. Graphics are used to

FIGURE **3.3.**

Cause-and-Effect Diagram for Improved Human Relations.

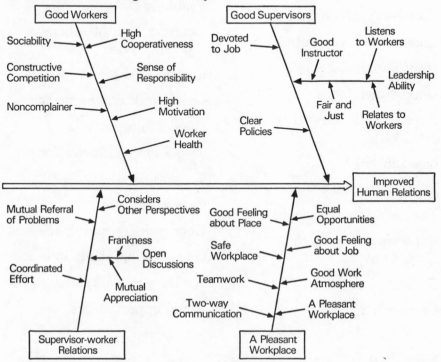

analyze the data, make management presentations, and act as an analysis aid.

All in all, the management presentation may be the most important part of the problem-solving process. It is simultaneously threatening to management and worker alike. In spite of training, management will be apprehensive about meeting with the workers, at least in the beginning. Workers will also experience anxiety about the meeting. It is important that both groups understand each others' concerns. However, it will fall to management to be most tolerant. Why? Because speaking before a group is the most feared of the common fears. Managers should be more comfortable at public speaking, having had more exposure and experience with it.

Case Studies—Some That Didn't Work

A midwest manufacturer of heavy equipment started a quality circle program to help reduce costs and improve quality of work life. The program administrator was given quality circles in addition to other duties. Attempts to sell the process to supervisors and workers were viewed as "just another *Personnel* program." As a result, line managers were reluctant to cooperate and allow time off for training. The absence of line-management support all but killed the effort. However, it was revitalized by assigning program responsibility to manufacturing upper managers. Supervisors were now less reluctant to cooperate with their line supervisors.

In a second case, a large northeastern service organization had quality circles functioning in all but one department. Tending towards an autocratic style, the department manager was nevertheless driven to circles by peer pressure. After training, the manager asked the pilot circle to come up with problems to work on. Continuing, he told the group that if they had any trouble deciding, he had a list of problems and suggested priorities. This continued until he told the group his choice of solution. Six weeks later the circle was nowhere to be found in that department.

A southeast manufacturer of auto parts did everything right, or so the company thought. Planning was detailed and flexible, training was widespread, select groups were chosen for start-up. However, the company neglected to involve the union leadership. Suspicions of the company's motives were spread to the rank and file. At first, members came late to circle meetings, then attendance declined, and finally attendance stopped. The word was out not to support a union-busting activity.

The final story takes place in an insurance company. Just like the previous case, the pilot circles were begun properly. The facilitator was deeply involved with each circle. Results were starting to show. Then the unexpected happened—the facilitator was transferred. The driving force was gone and things came to a grinding halt because the facilitator had run most of the meetings personally. The supervisors were being pressured by management for other things and so they had abdicated their role to the facilitator.

There are many more scenarios such as these. The next time you talk to a quality-circle consultant, ask for the less-than-successful stories. If he or she doesn't have any, consider looking elsewhere. However, there are thousands of positive stories. Stories that not only show returns as high as 8:1 but that have yielded improved communications, relaxed labor-management tensions, increased productivity and quality of work life, a more committed workforce, improved supervisory skills, and improved mutual respect and trust.

Involvement through Incentives

The General Accounting Office recently completed a study of incentive systems in use in American industry. Figure 3.4 shows that 80.6% of those surveyed found improved labor relations, 47.2% saw fewer grievances, and 36.1% experienced reduced absenteeism and turnover. The labor savings experienced by those surveyed varied widely and depended on the length of time in force. An average of 8.5% for firms with less than 5 years experience to 29% for those at it over 5 years for the most recent 5-year period. The savings were attributed to the following:

- Improved performance of employees.
- Change in employees' attitudes, job interest, and the like.
- Increased productivity.

FIGURE **3.4.**

Nonmonetary Benefits of Productivity-Sharing Programs.

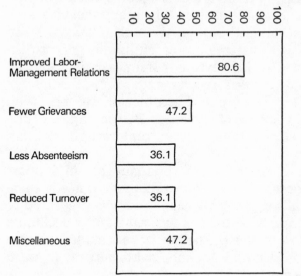

Percent of Productivity-Sharing Firms Reporting

Improved Labor-Management Relations 80.6

Fewer Grievances 47.2

Less Absenteeism 36.1

Reduced Turnover 36.1

Miscellaneous 47.2

- Reduction in scrap, rework, and waste.
- Better use of materials, supplies, and equipment.
- Cost-savings suggestions.
- Improved processes or procedures.
- Better product quality.

Incentives come in many forms but primarily cash, merchandise, and benefits. For the purpose of this book we will deal only with cash incentives. Specifically, we will look at individual and group-based incentives. However, one very important point must be made. Incentives by themselves will not significantly improve productivity. They must be backed by good quality of work life, capital, and research and development. Basic industries such as steel have found that even with incentives, productivity has declined without the backup systems. Finally, before you consider a new incentive system, look into what is currently in use. Build on that first. Make it work before a new one is introduced.

Suggestion Systems

In 1896 National Cash Register Co. started the first formalized suggestion system. Today there are over 6,000 systems involving over ten million workers. Unfortunately, many still view suggestion systems as an unused box on the wall (Figure 3.5). In fact, modern suggestion systems are carefully designed to encourage worker-supervisor interaction, communication, and involvement. Figure 3.6 shows a recommended flow chart for a suggestion system. The heavily outlined blocks are opportunities for worker-supervisor involvement in developing and presenting ideas, feedback on idea status, and recognition and awards presentation.

As is the case with any program, top-management support and commitment is essential. A suggestion system needs some form of reward to make it go. When this need was presented to the executive of a company whose system was rapidly declining, his comment was, "I don't see the necessity to include in such a program any rewards. Employees should be putting forward these ideas for the benefit of the company regardless of any reward."

The ultimate success of a suggestion system rests on the number of suggestions per 100 employees and the percentage of employees participating. The June, 1980, Annual Statistical Report of the National Association of Suggestion Systems (NASS)

FIGURE 3.5.

The Old Image of Suggestion Systems.

FIGURE 3.6.

Suggestion System Flow Chart.

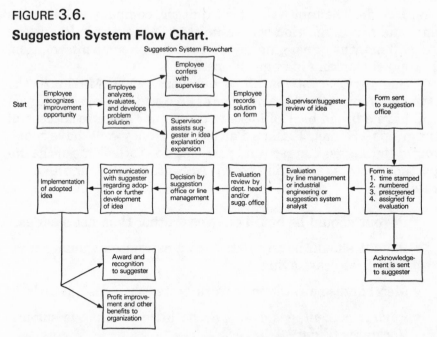

Source: *The Key Program for Maximum Suggestion Results.* National Association of Suggestion Systems, Chicago, 1977. Reprinted with permission.

shows the following averages for its nearly 6,000 plants, offices, field units, and federal government components:*

Total Suggestions Received	1,321,672
Total Suggestions Adopted	317,169
Adoption Rate	24%
Suggestions per 100 Eligible Employees	15
Percentage of Employees Submitting	12%
Total Awards paid	$50,277,480
Average Award	$ 159
Highest Award	$ 75,000
Average Net Savings per Adoption	$ 1,390
Net Savings per 100 Eligible Employees	$ 8,963

In addition to the obvious requirements for a successful system—top- and middle-management involvement, measurable goals, training, and the like—a rapid processing time is essential. Every effort should be made to keep the processing time under 90 days. If it exceeds 90 days you run the risk of creating a negative situation. For example, an employee of an insurance company described it this way: "I just received a check for a sugges-

---

*"Annual Statistical Report," National Association of Suggestion Systems, Chicago, IL, June 1980, p. 7.

tion I made. The funny thing is I quit the company two months ago, and my suggestion was submitted 18 months before I left. After 6 months of nagging my supervisor for some information, I stopped thinking of suggestions."

Suggestion systems are a numbers game. Maximize the number of inputs and the number of involved employees and you will have a broad base of ideas to draw on. The more successful programs—Kodak, Phillips Petroleum, Honeywell—have maximized the suggestion rate and participation rate. Some of the important factors, according to a NASS study, that improve the rates are:

- Payout should be based on gross rather than net savings.

- Payout should be calculated from estimated annual rather than first-year savings.

- Merchandise awards may work better than cash awards.

- Payout percentages over 20% do little to improve suggestion rates (Figure 3.7).

FIGURE 3.7.

Payout Percentage vs. Suggestion Rate.

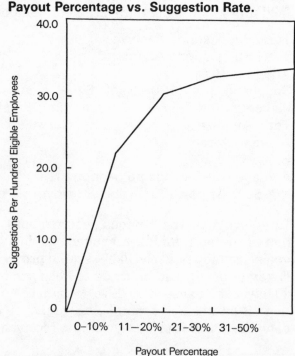

Payout Percentage

Source: National Association of Suggestion Systems, Chicago. Reprinted with permission.

- Anonymous systems have rates about half those that identify the suggester (Figure 3.8).

- Systems that provide for separate management input have twice the input rate and 65% more participation.

- Higher rates are found in systems administered by operating departments as compared to staff departments.

- Personal response at receipt, during evaluation, and at non-adoption notification provided doubled input and 50% improved participation over policies of written forms of contact.

- Presentation by the immediate supervisor showed at least a 15% improvement.

- Response time below 90 days provided 17% more suggestions per 100 eligible employees (Figure 3.9).

FIGURE **3.8.**

Suggestion and Participation Rate vs. Suggester Identification.

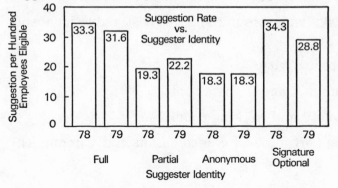

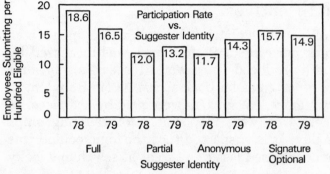

Source: National Association of Suggestion Systems, Chicago. Reprinted with permission.

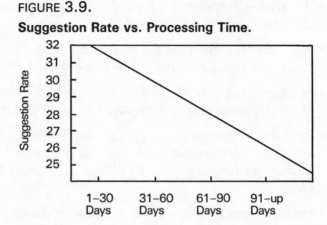

FIGURE 3.9.

Suggestion Rate vs. Processing Time.

Source: National Association of Suggestion Systems. Reprinted with permission.

Since most suggestion systems allow for input on a wide spectrum of operating matters, the benefits accrue to these areas:

- Product, task, and resource-specific cost reductions and avoidances.

- Increased productivity.

- Improved product and process quality.

- Improved safety and working conditions.

- Expanded opportunities for recognition and communications.

Individual Incentives

The oldest form of incentive plan has been direct payment to an individual for work performed. Performance was measured by the number of units produced—piecework. Piece-rate wages for cloth weaving are reported as far back as 604 B.C. in Babylon. In sixteenth-century Venice, oar makers were paid by the piece. In contrast, coworkers who were responsible for caulking ships were paid by the day. It is suspected that the logic behind this was that a broken oar posed less of a threat at sea than a leaky boat. This dichotomy of purpose supports the notion that piecework should be applied only to noncritical operations or parts.* Since World War II, the number of workers covered by piecework incentives has declined. A General Accounting Office study identified eight major reasons for the growing disenchantment.

1. Companies are not always able to maintain fair, equitable, and motivating incentive systems.

2. Workers resist new equipment or methods because of possible impact on their earnings, thus making the plan dysfunctional to the goal of productivity improvement.

3. Individual incentive plans may pit one employee against another, and if not adequately maintained can be a source of grievances.

4. The systems often ignore indirect workers and can create conflicts between them and those under the incentive plan.

5. Accurate maintenance of the standards is costly. Also, new tasks and processes can be a constant source of problems.

6. Since only labor costs are normally considered, material waste and inefficiency may actually increase.

7. Peer pressure, fear of upgraded standards, or other actions may restrict output.

8. The systems have less applicability as an organization moves toward more automation.†

Group Incentives

Group-incentive systems began in 1935. In that year Joseph Scanlon devised a plan that would save several near-bankrupt companies in the steel industry. The approach was based on sharing with labor the savings from reduced waste, improved ef-

---

*Carla S. O'Dell, *Gainsharing: Involvement, Incentives and Productivity,* American Management Associates, New York, 1981.

†"Productivity Sharing Programs: Can They Contribute to Productivity Improvement?" General Accounting Office, Report No. AFMD–81–22, March 3, 1981.

ficiency, and improved product quality. To obtain the savings, however, an organization needs people-oriented management and a mechanism of enlisting and using employee ideas. From this grew three other gainsharing methods: Rucker plans, Improshare, and profit sharing.

Profit sharing, unlike the Scanlon, Rucker, and Improshare plans, is based solely on the profits a company earns. The distribution of shares is made in cash to the employees or to an employee-deferred payment plan. Generally, the amount paid is usually limited by a combination of a minimum pretax profit base and a percentage of base wages. Since payments are tied to profits, they are usually distributed quarterly, semiannually, or annually. With payments based solely on profits, they can fluctuate through the effect of factors outside the control of the employees—accounting-procedure changes, market conditions, pricing policies, capital investment, and the like. Because of this and other factors, problems with profit-sharing plans include:

- The difficulty employees have relating to the system.

- Employees may look at payments as part of their earnings or as an entitlement.

- The lack of a tie between worker productivity and payments.

- The relatively low level of employee involvement.

The other three incentive systems go a long way toward encouraging employee involvement and tying individual effort to bonus payments. The Scanlon, Rucker, and Improshare systems, although substantially different in the way savings are calculated, are very similar.

- Payments are made regularly, usually monthly.

- Involvement and eligibility usually include all employees with the exception of senior management.

- Bonuses are based on the organization's output or production value rather than sales.

- Individual benefits are eliminated in favor of group incentives.

- Bonuses are most often distributed between the company and the employees on the basis of 25:75 for Scanlon and 50:50 for Rucker and Improshare.

- A portion of the employees' allocations is held in a reserve account for periods that would not normally have a bonus payment.

- Some form of suggestion system is used to channel and evaluate improvement ideas.

Some of these factors are shown comparatively in Table 3.2.

TABLE **3.2.**

A Comparison of Scanlon, Rucker, and Improshare.

	SCANLON	RUCKER	IMPROSHARE
1. Ideas channeled through a suggestion system	X	X	X
2. Employee involvement facilitated through committees	X	X	
3. Bonus frequency			
Monthly	X	X	
Weekly			X
4. Bonuses paid as a percent of earnings	X	X	X
5. Primary method of calculating bonus pools			
Total payroll costs as a percent of *net sales value of production*	X		
Total payroll costs as a percent of *net production value added*	X	X	
Total direct and indirect hours as percent of base-period standard hours			X
6. Bonus distribution (company:employees)			
25%:75%	X		
50%:50%		X	X
7. Reserves held for lean periods	X	X	
8. Eligibility (excluding senior management)			
Hourly	X	X	X
Salaried	X	X	X
Supervisory/management	X	X	X

The vehicle for inputing cost-savings ideas is a suggestion system. But, unlike the usual system, no individual awards are made. Rather, the savings accrue to a bonus pool which is later distributed. As a result, high adoption rates are common, standards are usually unchanged, and labor-cost reductions mean higher bonuses instead of layoffs.

The method of calculating the bonus pool to be distributed is the major distinction between the three plans. As shown in Table 3.2, Scanlon uses the net production sales value, Rucker the net production value added, and Improshare standard hours. Other approaches have been used in Scanlon plans including value added. Table 3.3 lists eleven different organizations with

TABLE 3.3.
Typical Organizations with Group Incentive Plans.

						MANAGEMENT STYLE			
COMPANY	PLAN	BEGAN	EMPLOYS	UNION Yes/No	PRODUCTS OR INDUSTRY	AUTOCRATIC	PATERNALISTIC	CONSULTATIVE	1978 BONUS
American Darling Valve	Scanlon	1978	400	Y	Valves, fire hydrants		P		5%
Atwood Vacuum Co.	Scanlon	1954	2200	Y	Automatic equipment			C	21%
Coast Catamaran	Improshare	1978	200	N	Boating	A			10%
Colonial Manufacturing Co.	Scanlon	1970	250	N	Grandfather clocks		P		13%
Eckstrom Industries	Improshare	1978	55	N	Electrical meter socket adapters		P		6%
Gast Manufacturing	Improshare	1973	400	N	Compressors, vacuum pumps	A			14%
Herman Miller	Scanlon	1950	1540	N	Office furniture			C	5%
Parker Pen Co.	Scanlon	1954	1000	Y	Writing instruments			C	16%
Presto-Lite (Alabama)	Scanlon	1978	675	N	Solenoids, alternators			C	16%
Presto-Lite (Oklahoma)	Improshare	1978	320	N	DC motors for auto and marine equipment	A			8%

Source: *Productivity Incentives Workshop* (Houston: American Productivity Center, 1980).

active group-incentive programs. Its purpose is to demonstrate the range of sizes, products, management styles, and bonuses that can be utilized in incentive plans.

Calculating the Scanlon Bonus Pool

To calculate the bonus pool, a threshold value, or base ratio, must be determined. Payments to the pool are made only when the expended labor is *below* this value. Historical accounting and cost data are usually used to determine this base ratio which is expressed as follows:

$$\text{Base Ratio} = \frac{\text{Total Payroll Costs}}{\text{Net Sales Value of Production}}$$

Let's go back to the Dig Deep Construction Company data to calculate the Scanlon bonus for 1982 (Table 2.10).

The base ratio would be calculated as follows:

$$\frac{\text{Total Labor Cost 1977–1981}}{\text{Total Sales 1977–1981}} = \frac{18,000,000}{206,800,000}$$

Base Ratio = .087

Therefore, for 1982 the calculations would be:

January, 1982, sales	$4,580,000
Less allowances, discounts, etc.	(215,000)
Net sales for January, 1982	$4,365,000
Inventory adjustment	62,500
Net sales value of production	$4,427,500
Threshold total labor cost ($\times$ .087)	385,193
Actual total labor cost	337,253
Total to bonus pool	47,940
Company share at 25%	11,985
Employee share at 75%	35,955
Employee share to reserve ($\times$ .25)	8,989
January bonus to employees	26,966
Bonus as percent of total labor cost	8.0%

Calculating the Rucker Bonus

The threshold value in this plan is called the Rucker standard; it is calculated by dividing the total payroll cost by the net production value added in a base period. Using Table 2.10 again, the Rucker ratio could be calculated as follows:

1981 net sales	$46,800,000
Less allowances, etc.	(2,600,000)
Inventory adjustments	750,000
Net value of production	44,950,000
Less total purchases	32,500,000
Net production value added	12,450,000

$$\text{Rucker Standard} = \frac{\text{Total Labor Cost}}{\text{Production Value Added}}$$

$$\text{Rucker Standard} = \frac{4,700,000}{12,450,000} = .3775$$

Therefore, any time the monthly ratio falls below .3775, a bonus payment is made. So for January, 1982, the Rucker bonus calculation might look like this:

January, 1982, sales	$4,580,000
Less allowances	(215,000)
Inventory adjustments	62,500
Net sales value of production	4,427,500
Less total purchases	3,501,500
Net production value added	926,000
Rucker Standard labor cost ($\times$ 0.3775)	349,565
Actual total labor cost	337,253
Total to bonus pool	12,312
Amount to reserve account (25%)	3,078
Amount distributed	$ 9,234

Calculating the Improshare Bonus

Improshare (an acronym for IMproved PROductivity through SHARing), unlike the other two plans, is based on the labor content of individual products and a base-labor productivity value defined as the ratio of the total labor-hour content to the total standard-value hours. Assume there are 25 production and 15 nonproduction workers producing 1,000 of product X and 500 of product Y. The calculation of the base period standard value would be as follows:

$$\text{Work hour standard} = \frac{\text{Total Production Work Hours}}{\text{Quantity Produced}}$$

$$\text{For Product } X = \frac{15 \text{ employees} \times 40 \text{ hours}}{1,000 \text{ units}} = 0.6 \text{ hours per piece}$$

$$\text{For Product } Y = \frac{10 \text{ employees} \times 40 \text{ hours}}{500 \text{ units}} = 0.8 \text{ hours per piece}$$

Total standard value hours = $(0.6 \times 1,000) + (0.8 \times 500)$
Total standard value hours = $\underline{1,000}$

From this we can calculate the Base Productivity Factor, *BPF*.

$$BPF = \frac{\text{Total labor hour content}}{\text{Total standard value hours}}$$

$$BPF = \frac{\text{Production Employee Hours} + \text{Nonproduction Employee Hours}}{1,000}$$

$$BPF = \frac{(25 + 15) \, 40 \text{ hours}}{1,000 \text{ Hours}} = 1.6$$

The next step is to calculate the bonus percentage for a given month based on the actual hours vs. the calculated standard hours. If for January, 1982, the product output was 1,200 of product X and 400 of product Y, the bonus would be calculated as follows:

Product X = 0.6 hours/unit × 1,200 units × 1.6 = 1,152 hours
Product Y = 0.8 hours/unit ×   400 units × 1.6 =   512 hours
  Standard hours for units produced 1,664
  Actual hours worked $\underline{1,495}$
  Net hours saved $\underline{\underline{169}}$

If labor savings are shared equally, the employee bonus percentage is calculated by:

$$\text{Employee Bonus Percent} = \frac{50\% \text{ of Hours Saved}}{\text{Total Actual Hours}} \times 100$$

$$\text{Employee Bonus} = \frac{84.5}{1,495} = \underline{\underline{5.65\%}}$$

As we saw earlier, many benefits can come from a group-incentive program. But what about the start-up cost? Here are seven you have to think about before committing to a program.

1. A significant amount of management time will be needed.

2. Committee activities will eat up a lot of time.

3. A broad awareness, education, and training process is needed.

4. New employees at all levels will need indoctrination.

5. A production-cost system capable of timely, accurate data will be necessary.

6. Some managers will have to change their style and attitude to be more participative.

7. You can expect to engage a consultant for the design and implementation assistance.

Nonmonetary Returns

A 1975 study by the Old National Commission on Productivity and Work Quality into the type and frequency of plan suggestions showed some interesting results. In the first three months of a new program, a large number of ideas and suggestions dealt with complaints about the working conditions and environment. As shown in Figure 3.10, this was reduced substantially by year end. As the number of suggestions increase, the organization may not be able to respond quickly enough. This can send negative signals back to the employees. However, these start-up pains are quickly dissipated.

Over time, the number of suggestions remain high with continued input to working conditions, safety, production quantity, product quality, and cost reduction. As shown in Figure 3.11,

FIGURE 3.10.

Type of Suggestion and Degree of Participation Over Time.

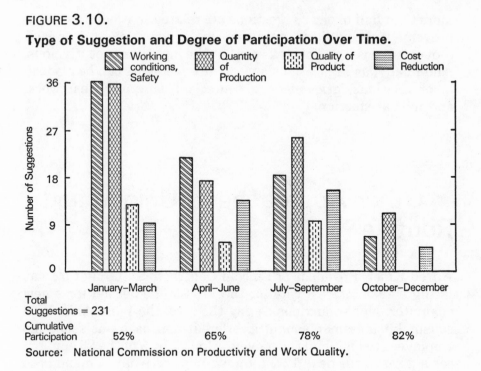

Total
Suggestions = 231

Cumulative
Participation   52%   65%   78%   82%

Source: National Commission on Productivity and Work Quality.

FIGURE 3.11.

Type of Suggestion.

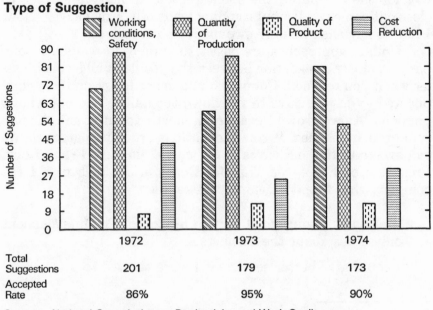

Total
Suggestions   201   179   173

Accepted
Rate   86%   95%   90%

Source: National Commission on Productivity and Work Quality.

more than half of the suggestions are related to productivity improvement. In addition, note the acceptance rate—86% to 90% —over three years. This tells us that the inputs are not frivolous. And finally, as Figure 3.4 showed, improvements can be made in labor relations, grievances, absenteeism, turnover, teamwork, and job satisfaction.

Other Approaches—Unique and Routine

Alfred Knief, President of Lincoln Contractors Supply Co., was facing a 16% interest rate for the $70,000 he needed for a new computer. Not so anxious to pay the rate, the West Allis, Wisconsin, businessman sought a different approach—he asked his employees to lend him the money. Almost 75% of the 23 employees agreed to the deal: 12% interest on a three-day demand note with no penalties. With individual loans ranging between $1,000 and $20,000, a total of $109,000 was raised. This was enough to pay for the computer, the software, and to leave a surplus to close out some smaller outstanding loans. Mr. Knief says, "Now, I like to say that we only owe money to ourselves."*

Unique approaches are easier to employ in a smaller company. A closer association between the people at all levels is easier when you're small. Communications are faster and less complicated—you just have to yell down the hall to find out what's going on. As we grow larger communications suffer and the personal touch declines. If communications are left to atrophy, we can awake to find ourselves in difficult situations. Frank Ruck, President of Employer Transfer Corporation, tells of a large company that found its employees saying:

- We're not giving good service anymore. The management only cares about the numbers.

- I could give better service, if I were allowed to.

---

*With the permission of *Inc.* Magazine, April 1981, p. 28.

- Management never asks my opinion about anything.

- The management really doesn't care about people like they used to; they're not concerned about me as a person.*

In an attempt to identify some of these concerns, some companies use a suggestion-box system. Employees are encouraged to ask questions, make suggestions, or voice concerns over anything about the company, from safety, to overtime abuses, to waste reduction, to "sex in the parking lot." Most suggestions, however, act as a vent and thus serve a real purpose. The activity is directly dependent on how each input is handled. As we saw with suggestion systems, the rate of activity depends on several factors. Well-run systems may manage 10 inputs per month. But when it comes to communications to generate involvement, nothing beats eye-to-eye techniques, especially if they are handled right and in small groups. To handle it right consider the following:

- Don't use it as a fad, you fool no one.
- Be prepared to work at it for a year.
- Don't stifle discussions of any subject.
- Keep the meeting informal and friendly.
- Use round-table settings for meeting.
- Off-site meetings can stimulate new ideas.
- Focus on objectives, not personalities.
- Insure continuous feedback.
- Establish an agenda.

Let's look at a couple of cases. Both companies have 150–200 employees, are nonunion, and have similar growth patterns. One manufactures pharmaceuticals, the other paper pulp.

In the pharmaceutical company, the president held semimonthly meetings with selected employees. Care was taken to avoid subordinate/supervisor combinations. The format of the

---

*Ruck, Frank J. Jr., "Productivity Doesn't Just Happen," CNA 17th Annual Executive Conference, Chicago, IL, September 10, 1981.

meeting was simple. The president reported on the latest business developments and new products. The meeting then turned toward the discussion of problems. After some initial successes the time between meetings began to increase. Eventually, after a year, the program ceased. Three reasons were identified: 1) middle managers were not included; 2) improvements were capital intensive and not readily implementable; and 3) follow up was lacking. In the second case, meetings were run by the general manager. Attendees were representatives of the various departments, elected by each department's personnel. Salary, hourly, and management personnel were represented. Productivity was up 45% by the end of the second year. Follow up, action plans, and responsibility assignments were key factors in each monthly meeting. Subjects ranged from lost contracts, to long-range plans, to quality problems, to customer complaints. Each representative was responsible for informing his or her department about these various problems and actions and to bring back ideas and suggestions.

Some Cautions

The cautions, problems, and benefits of employee involvement have been fairly well covered in this chapter. Employee involvement is not a simple process or a quick one. Whichever technique you may select, you cannot spend too much time on the preparation and planning stages before implementation. The same is true about feedback and maintenance afterward. However, a new problem is peeking around the corner. With all the emphasis on first-level employees—white and blue collar—what is happening to the attitudes of the managers? Since 1950, Opinion Research Corporation has been studying the shifting patterns in attitude between managers, clerical employees, and hourly employees.[*]

The hierarchy gap—the difference between management attitudes and hourly/clerical attitudes—is narrowing. This is espe-

---

[*]M. R. Cooper, B. S. Morgan, P. M. Foley, L. B. Kaplan, "Changing Employee Values: Deepening Discontent?" *Harvard Business Review*, Jan.–Feb., 1979.

cially true about a company's willingness to listen to problems and complaints. The most recent data show the following percent of respondents who rated their organization "good" or "very good":

Period	Managers	Clerical	Hourly*
1960	70	28	22
1960–64	53	29	13
1965–69	52	37	43
1970–74	49	42	32
1975–77	55	38	29
1977	50	42	35

These data show a hierarchy gap reduction of nearly 50% in just 17 years. What should be of concern is the answer to two questions:

1. Is the increase for clerical and hourly employees a result of increased employee involvement and quality-of-work-life programs?

2. Is the decline in manager opinions due to the feeling of neglect by these same programs?

If the answers are positive, we could be heading for big problems with managers by the end of the 1980s. The reason is that employee involvement and quality-of-work-life programs are just starting to build and spread. A hint of this is supported by a 60% reduction in the gap for rating a company's efforts at doing something about employees' problems and complaints.

> IF YOU EMBARK ON AN EMPLOYEE INVOLVEMENT PROGRAM, DON'T IGNORE THE MANAGERS.

In fact, consider introducing some form of assessment of the managers' attitudes in order to head off problems.

---

*Cooper et al., "Changing Employee Values."

Summary

The greatest advances in productivity will come from within the organization. However, that improvement will require changes and innovations in our treatment of people—the human resources of an organization. The needs of these resources are changing and we as managers must change with them. Just like the captain of a ship, we cannot change the direction or force of the wind, but we can certainly adjust our sails to accommodate it. As C. Jackson Grayson, Chairman of the American Productivity Center, points out, "Autocratic, bureaucratic organizations in business and public service have suppressed the desires and abilities of the individual to feel that he or she is contributing."* Management has failed to keep pace with the changes in the workforce.

There is no doubt that it is more difficult to manage today than it was 2000 years ago or even fifty years ago. Twenty centuries ago the workforce was slave labor whose motivation was to do what was asked or to be killed. Fifty or so years ago, workers were also motivated by survival, but of a different sort—they were plagued by war, depression, starvation. Today, we need to manage *for* motivation—a much more difficult task to perform.

Studies at General Motors have shown that productivity and quality of work life are linked. Arguing in favor of one over the other is a little like arguing about which hand makes the noise when you clap. What is important is that we recognize that "the oncoming generation have new doubts about the ideals of efficiency. They are unwilling to pay the crushing price of loss of pride, mind-killing monotony, dehumanization and stress diseases in return for the highest wages in history."† Or, perhaps it is even more basic. Could it be that "there's every reason to believe that industrial society, a relative innovation, is simply unnatural from a biological point of view? Man got along for 2000 years in an agricultural society. Then he was following a natural cycle. Now he just works himself to death, breaks it periodically with a vacation, and the rest of the time gets bored and has the impression of never getting anywhere."‡

Employee involvement works toward overcoming these problems in a way that is natural to the social animal that is man.

---

*Personal communication.

†E. L. Cass and F. G. Zimmer, *Man and Work in Society,* New York: Van Nostrand, 1976.

‡D. Jenkins, *Job Power,* New York: Doubleday, 1973, p. 41.

CHAPTER 4

"Would you tell me please,
which way I ought to go from
here?"

"That depends a good deal on
where you want to get to," said the
cat.

"I don't much care where—,"
said Alice.

"Then it doesn't matter which
way you go," said the cat.

—LEWIS CARROLL

Source: Lewis Carroll, *Alice's Adventures in Wonderland* (New York: Delacorte Press, 1977).

Opportunities to Improve Productivity

What the Surveys Reveal

To better understand the major obstacles that hinder productivity improvement, ask a number of managers their opinions about the subject. Several dozen middle managers from around the country, representing a broad spectrum of company sizes and industries, were asked that during the American Productivity Center's seminar, "Productivity Improvement: Planning, Managing, and Measuring." Judging from the frequency and ranking provided by the managers, the following eight items group the primary obstacles to productivity from the perspective of mid-level managers.

1. *Productivity Management.* Excessive apathy or complacency concerning the need to improve productivity and a lack of commitment or involvement to a well-planned and organized effort. Another management factor mentioned was the absence of clear, well-defined productivity-improvement goals.

2. *Productivity Planning.* An uncoordinated shotgun approach was a significant planning deficiency. Another was the blind *adoption* of techniques without sufficient *adaptation* to the individual organization and its environment. A final point was the unrealistic expectations of managers about timing and amount of results.

3. *Communications.* Although frequently mentioned, it was not well defined by the participants. Some specifics that fell in this category included comments related to: current business situations, availability of top management, too much dependence on memos, no opportunity to contribute and be heard, and the need for more dialogue rather than a series of one-way conversations.

4. *Incentives.* Most managers felt that there was no incentive to improve productivity. Their reward systems were based on short-term results rather than the long-term benefits of productivity efforts. Therefore, they tend not to give it much effort. Similarly, if they do not share in the benefits and savings of productivity improvement, they will be less than enthusiastic with their support. This is often aggravated by upper-management pressures for rapid results— frequently at the expense of long-term performance.

5. *Insufficient Involvement.* The involvement of middle- and upper-level managers in the planning and implementation phases of a productivity-improvement effort is considered vital to its success. Only after this is achieved can involvement be successfully extended to the first levels of the organization.

6. *Awareness.* Many employees lack understanding of how productivity improvements can increase job security, competitiveness, and the long-term health of a company.

7. *Management Style.* Autocratic management was the style most often noted as an obstacle. While this style may be necessary at times, it should not dominate. Participants read into autocratic management a lack of trust, poor communications, nonsupportiveness, and a lack of involvement in decision making.

8. *Resistance to Change.* Resistance to change is undoubtedly an obstacle to improving productivity. Productivity improvement requires a change in the way we do things. The resistance is likely due to misunderstanding, lack of incentives, discomfort with something new, overemphasis on the short-term, or any one of a number of other factors. Another contributing factor is the absence of a practical, integrated productivity-improvement approach.

Following these eight items was a collection of other thoughts, ranging from supervisory skills to lack of productivity expertise, insufficient time, restrictive labor-contract requirements, and lack of resources.

While this survey is admittedly informal and unscientific, it does exhibit some interesting results. And, when compared to more professional and highly structured surveys, the results have strong areas of agreement. The Gray-Judson Survey* of top management, and the U. S. Chamber of Commerce's survey of workers, show that there are several areas of potential improvement. These opportunities are all valid. However, their importance depends on one's perspective—top management, middle management, or worker.

The Gray-Judson Survey included 178 top executives from 160 industrial firms representing over three-dozen industries. The survey, conducted between June, 1980, and August, 1981, included chief executive and operating officers, presidents, and their direct reports. Of the organizations included, 39% were in the Fortune 500, over half had sales over $110 million, and 28% had sales below $50 million (Table 4.1). Of the organizations surveyed, almost three-quarters reported productivity improvements of 10% or less, while 22% did not know what their productivity performance had been. Only 4% indicated productivity advances of over 10%. However, the numbers do not reflect the reality of the situation. Since most of the reporting companies were not using deflated figures, it is suspected that as much as 40% of the organizations may have actually had productivity declines.

The survey was conducted by asking the respondents to select from a list of 16 options the 5 that contributed most to past productivity-improvement successes. In addition, they were asked to select 5 that were responsible for disappointments. The responses are shown in Figure 4.1. The survey respondents identified capital investment, top-management commitment, financial controls and systems, middle managers, communications, and employee relations as the primary reasons for past

TABLE 4.1.

Gray-Judson Survey of Executives.

	RESPONDENTS	
COMPANY SIZE	NUMBER	PERCENT
Fortune 500 listed companies	63	39%
Others with sales over $110 million	24	15
Sales between $50 million and $110 million	29	18
Sales between $10 million and $50 million	44	28
	160	100

Source: Gray-Judson, Inc., Boston, MA.

---

*Data supplied courtesy of Arnold S. Judson, Chairman, Gray-Judson, Inc., Boston, MA, December, 1981.

FIGURE **4.1.**

Frequency of Causes of Past Productivity-Improvement Successes and Disappointments.

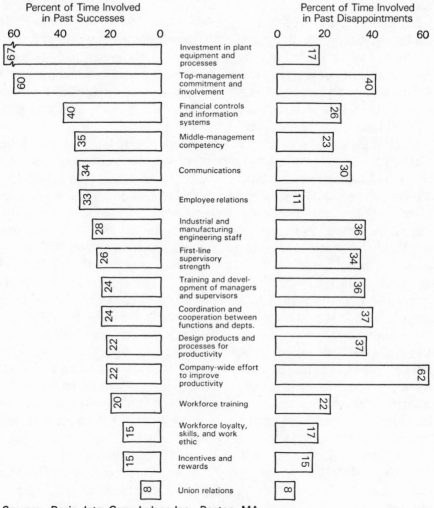

Source: Basic data: Gray-Judson Inc., Boston, MA.

productivity improvements. On the other hand, disappointments were laid at the doorstep of piecemeal, unplanned approaches to improving productivity, the absence of top-management support, inadequate interfunctional cooperation and coordination, followed by insufficient designing of products and processes for productivity improvement, insufficient management and supervisory training and development, and questionable industrial and manufacturing engineering capabilities.

It is easy to see how the *causes,* whether present or absent, may have contributed to successful or disappointing results.

While many of the causes are not surprising, a few of the relative positions and weights may be. For example, it appears that incentives/rewards and union relations do not play a significant role in either the successes or disappointments. A 1981 U. S. Chamber of Commerce survey reinforced the low significance of union relations but disagreed considerably with the role of incentives and rewards.* This dichotomy is likely a result of the degree and level of participation in incentive and reward systems with respect to base earnings between the executives and workers. A more complete discussion of the Chamber's study is presented later in this section.

Two other interesting observations about the Gray-Judson study are the role of top management involvement and the need for broad-based productivity-improvement plans and activities. These subjects are discussed in detail in Chapters III and V, respectively, but nevertheless warrant some additional comments.

Top-management support, involvement, and commitment are vital to a successful effort. If lower levels of the organization perceive only lip service from above, they will not give the activity a fair share of effort. Why should they dilute their performance on activities that bear little interest to those above? One way to demonstrate interest and commitment is by establishing a company-wide productivity-improvement strategy. As the survey showed, this approach was not the most significant factor in successful programs but it certainly was in the disappointing ones. Besides, its cost is substantially lower than an investment approach and will uncover improvements from many more areas than any organization could ever hope to reach with significant investments. This is primarily true in the human resource arena—particularly the white-collar and knowledge workers.

The role management plays in the improvement effort is demonstrated by some of the other statistics developed by the survey.

- Approximately 9 out of 10 executives indicated that productivity improvement was accomplished through cost savings focused mostly on manufacturing.

- Less than 2 in 10 paid any attention to the interactions between marketing, sales, engineering, finance, personnel, manufacturing, and other white-collar and knowledge workers.

Management Attitudes Toward Productivity, Chamber of Commerce of the United States, Washington, DC, 1981.

- Only 25% stated that productivity-improvement strategies were company-wide.

- Less than a third required detailed productivity plans and objectives or expected managers to spend much time at developing them.

- Where productivity plans were used, less than half the executives required them to support and be consistent with other business plans.

- Almost all the productivity-improvement efforts were uncoordinated and addressed symptoms rather than causes. And three quarters of these efforts had life expectancies of less than one year.

While these are the views of top and middle managers, what about the man on the street—the "average worker"? Well, a 1980 study, "Workers' Attitudes Toward Productivity," conducted by The Gallup Organization for the U. S. Chamber of Commerce, showed that the attitudes and abilities of the workers themselves and their managers offered the opportunity ". . . to bring about the *largest improvement* in performance and productivity in most companies."* Of a list of 9 improvement opportunities, the survey's 800-plus respondents were asked to select the 2 most important opportunities. The following shows the 9 items in order of frequency each was selected by those surveyed.

Opportunities for the Largest Productivity Improvement in Most Companies

Workers' attitudes and abilities	53%
Management attitudes and abilities	37%
Supervisors' attitudes and abilities	21%
Quality of tools and equipment	21%
Amount of innovation and new technology	18%
Government rules and regulations	12%
Union practices	10%
Amount of investment in new plant and equipment	9%
Availability and use of computers	6%

---

*R. H. Clarke and J. R. Morris, *Workers' Attitudes Toward Productivity,* Chamber of Commerce of the United States, Washington, DC, 1980.

When posed a similar question regarding what "... is most important to you about the job you have," the order of preference was as listed below. Also shown was the "second most important."

	Most Important	Second Most
Job Security (knowing that I will not be laid off).	30%	14%
The *Satisfaction* I get from my work.	24%	19%
Money; salary.	22%	32%
The *Quality* of the work I do.	17%	21%
Chance for a *Promotion* to a better job.	5%	12%

While job security is a primary concern to workers, money is a strong second, followed by job satisfaction and the quality of the job performed. Some more interesting conclusions can be drawn from the other questions in the surveys concerning the attitudes that workers have toward their jobs.

- 70% feel enthusiatic and optimistic about doing a good job.

- 84% believe that more involvement in decisions that affect their jobs will result in their working harder and doing better.

- 83% believe hard work makes at least some difference to the success of their companies.

- 60% would like to become more involved in helping other people do their best.

- 48% think that hard work and doing your best results in recognition and better jobs.

If we take the high points of these three surveys, the focus is on top management, a coordinated productivity-improvement effort, communications, employee involvement, capital investment, and the skills, attitudes, and abilities of all employees from the top to the first level. Table 4.2 shows a listing of the 11 factors that appear to be present, in one form or another, in the three studies. The listing is in order of weighted importance

TABLE 4.2.

Key Factors to Improve Productivity From the Perspective of Top and Middle Managers and Workers.

	TOP MANAGEMENT	MIDDLE MANAGEMENT	WORKERS
Management interest, commitment, and involvement	H	H	M
Clear company productivity-improvement plans and objectives	H	H	M
Communications	M	H	H
Employee involvement	M	M	H
Investment in plant, equipment processes, technology, etc.	H	M	L
Top and middle management skills, attitudes, and abilities	M	M	M
First-line supervisory skills, attitudes, and abilities	M	M	M
Incentives and awards	L	M	H
Worker attitudes, skills, loyalty	L	L	H
Training of managers, supervisors, and the workforce	M	M	L
Union and employee relations	L	M	L

Note: The order of preference was established by assigning a value of 5, 3, or 1, to the ratings of High, Medium, or Low in each category of management and workers. The total point score was then used to establish the order.

within each group. Weighting was accomplished by assigning an arbitrary value of 5, 3, or 1 to the levels of importance of high, moderate, and low, respectively. The sums of these weights were then used to establish the rank order.

The data from the surveys just described provide many areas that have the potential for generating productivity improvements. But these are of course generalizations; not all may apply to your specific organization. And those that do must be looked at more closely. The remainder of this chapter deals with various techniques that will help a manager assess opportunities for improving productivity. Perhaps even more importantly in some cases, the methods can provide a red flag that there is a potential productivity problem that needs closer examination. This can then be followed by other auditing approaches. Most of the auditing methods can be condensed into four primary categories: productivity measurement, nominal group processes, structured interviews, and questionnaires. Each will be discussed in detail and illustrated with case studies.

Improvement Opportunities Through Measurement

As we saw in Chapter II, productivity-measurement systems can add substantially to the manager's ability to analyze a business's past and future. However, a major shortcoming arises when we attempt to apply the measures to lower levels of the organization—specifically, to the first-line supervisory and worker levels. The major reason is the difficulty in relating the measures to the jobs that are performed by the individuals and organizational groups. Therefore, different measurement systems were introduced—interrelated partial measures, work sampling, and structured brainstorming. Structured brainstorming is dealt with in great detail in the next section.

As we saw in Chapter II, productivity measurement provides an indication of a company's well being. But, without exception, only trends are indicated, not causes of problems. To obtain a readout of causes, more detective work is needed. The Dig Deep Construction Company was seeing internal labor costs increase and capital expenditures decrease. The result was increased profits through price increases rather than higher productivity. The Fast Food Emporium showed similar results, except for energy productivity. There are many possible reasons for the two companies' decline. The Fast Food Emporium was experiencing increased waste and employee consumption, and the Dip Deep Construction Company was fighting increased wages without offsetting productivity increases or increased capital investment. On the other hand, Boston Edison's declining labor productivity was caused by a decrease in electrical demand rather than by less efficient and/or effective labor.

What actions can be taken once the problem area is identified are as varied as the causes. For example, Dig Deep may want to reassess its overhead manning levels or introduce a minicomputer to handle many of the cost-control and scheduling functions now performed manually. The Fast Food Emporium can reduce scrap losses by improved cooking schedules. It can reduce worker consumption by forbidding it or by controlling it with a "chit" system where each employee would be given a fixed number of chits for various foods he or she wishes to eat during the week. In the case of a utility, efforts to expand the number of users is quite limited. Therefore, efforts directed at capital utilization, maintenance, and other support functions may be more fruitful.

Case No. 1—The Order-entry Department

On the departmental level, productivity measures are also used to evaluate improvement opportunities. Figure 2.19 showed the productivity of an order-entry department of a medium-sized manufacturer. As we saw earlier, productivity in 1979 and 1980 increased over 1978 by 13.7% and 11.2%, respectively. However, from 1979 to 1980, productivity dropped 2.3%. The reason was a reduction in sales of $200,000 and an increase in department personnel from 14 to 16. Upon further investigation, it was found that the additional personnel were added to the clerical support staff. Now the problem was to determine the rationale behind the additional people and to look for ways of changing back to the original manning level. In this particular case, the clerical additions were caused by an increase in the number of orders, each listing more items. Thus, more clerical time was needed to prepare, acknowledge, and process the orders. In addition, more line items also meant more individual shop orders and shipping releases to the warehouse—and more time spent at the copy machine.

Following a series of discussions with employees of the department, an analysis of the work flow, and determining causes for the various job tasks and requirements, several improvements were instituted.

1. A copy machine was obtained and dedicated to the department. This eliminated time lost in travel and waiting. Annual Savings: 1,000 hours.

2. Noncritical or long lead-time items were held and consolidated before release to the shop. Annual Savings: 1,500 hours.

3. Warehouse items were listed in a sequence closely related to their order on the shelves. Annual Savings: none for order entry; 750 hours in the warehouse.

Case No. 2.—Construction Productivity Slips

Work-sampling studies of construction personnel at major utility power plants were showing continued decline. Less than 50% of the workday was spent doing the jobs the workers were being paid to do—weld, haul, string wire, run cranes, pour concrete. In some cases the productivity had fallen to just over 26%, meaning that people were only working at their assigned tasks for about two hours each day. The causes came from several sources, the biggest of which was management itself. Poor scheduling and job-site logistics, coupled with weather fluctuations, were primary causes for the decline.

Much time was lost when workers needed to use the sanitary facilities, or protect themselves from wind and cold, or redo work, or search for equipment another work shift had changed or borrowed. For large projects, an improvement of only 10% would translate into tens of thousands of dollars, all of which go directly to the bottom line. These savings do not always come from reduced labor, however. Substantial savings can come from lower interest payments on construction loans if the project is completed ahead of schedule (or not as late as expected.)

The recommendations for improvements covered many areas. Expected annual savings could exceed $100,000.

1. Increase the number of portable sanitary facilities and place them closer to the work areas.

2. Increase the number and availability of tools and materials to reduce intershift competition for them.

3. Erect wind screens to reduce the wind-chill factor.

4. Increase the involvement of field managers in the planning and scheduling phases of the projects.

5. Introduce a supervisory and management-skills training program in the field to overcome communications and interpersonal skill deficiencies.

The final productivity-measurement based approach to assessing opportunities to improve productivity was developed by IBM Corporation in the mid-1960s.* Known as the Common Staffing System, it was developed to measure productivity trends and differences in the indirect work force across the organization. The system has been used in three primary ways: 1) to provide a basis of comparing productivity, 2) to be an input source for estimating manpower needs for new plants and products, and 3) to evaluate productivity trends in the organization. By combining the first and third items, an approach for auditing man-

---

Productivity Improvement: Planning, Managing, and Measuring, American Productivity Center, Houston, TX, 1982.

ning levels and resource utilization was made possible. To see how this works, let's walk through an example.

Consider a medium-sized printing company with twelve printing plants around the country. Upper management is interested in evaluating opportunities for improving productivity of support functions at each plant. It also wants to know whether plants have been successful in improving productivity and which ones may need help. As a starting point, the maintenance function will be analyzed. Since all the plant operations are similar, but differ only in size, it is decided to look at the number of people engaged in maintaining the facilities and equipment as a function of plant size in thousands of square feet. The data for the twelve plants are listed below and are shown in Figure 4.2.

Plant Size	Maintenance Personnel
20	8
36	7
108	11
40	5
100	10
72	9
110	12
60	6
90	9
80	8
120	9
60	10

The trend line in the graph is fitted to the points but *is not* a least squares' fit. A least squares' fit would not have passed through the origin, the 0,0 point on the graph. Rather, it would have intersected the vertical axis at 2 people for a zero square foot plant. Since this is illogical, the line is force fitted through 0,0, the origin. To accomplish this, the line joins the origin and a point representing the average number of maintenance personnel per plant (8.7) and the average plant size (74,700 square feet). A least squares' regression analysis would not improve accuracy enough to warrant its use. In addition, it might add an element of complexity unnecessary for analysis.

With the data in this format, let's look at the New York plant as shown in Figure 4.2. This plant employs seven people to

FIGURE 4.2.

Interplant Comparison of Maintenance Personnel vs. Plant Area.

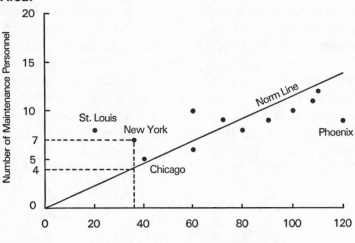

Plant Area in Thousands of Square Feet

maintain a plant of 36,000 sq. ft. However, the trend line indicates that this size plant should employ only four in the maintenance function. The Chicago plant, with 40,000 sq. ft., is pretty close to the trend line. Although New York appears to be too high, it may be appropriate according to the age of the equipment or type of paper and other materials being used. It does warrant asking the question, "What is the reason for Chicago's being closer to the line than New York?" and, "What can Chicago learn from New York?" Similar questions can be asked about the St. Louis and Phoenix plants with respect to the norm—both positive and negative. If St. Louis is overmanned, maintenance costs may be higher than necessary. On the other hand, if Phoenix is understaffed, maintenance labor will be low but plant-capacity utilization may suffer from high down-time along with increased scrap rates.

The last piece of information needed is related to the trend for each plant. This can be accomplished by comparing the actual manning level to the norm for two or more successive periods. If the New York plant showed an initial ratio of people to area of,

Manning Ratio $= \dfrac{36}{7} = 5.14$, and

after some time this was improved by reducing the number of maintenance staff to six, the ratio would by $36/6 = 6.00$. The resulting improvement is calculated as follows:

$$\text{Productivity Index} = \frac{\text{Manning Ratio in Period 2}}{\text{Manning Ratio in Period 1}} = \frac{6.00}{5.14}$$

Productivity Index = 1.167,

an improvement of 16.7%. Chicago, however, may have gone from four to five people—a decline of 20%. These percentages are indications of changes—the magnitudes are not absolute. This system, then, like other measurement approaches, is based more on consistency than absolute accuracy. Therefore, the combination of change and the relative position of a function to the norm line provides a hint of potential problems and/or opportunities for improvement.

With data collected for a number of activities within each function, a clear picture of the total organization would emerge. To do this requires an analysis of the organization's functions, work activities, and the causes for these activities. Figure 4.3 shows a simplified listing of these for our printing-company ex-

FIGURE 4.3.

Functions, Activities, and Work Causes.

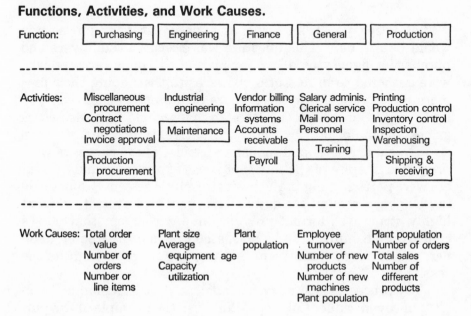

ample. Each business function has several activities that are conducted within it. A complication arises, though, when the activities are split between two or more departments. For example, training may be conducted in engineering and production. Both efforts would have to be aggregated. In addition, a work cause may be related to more than one activity such as plant population and the number of orders. By collecting data on activity/cause pairs, aggregating them within functions, and comparing across organizational lines will highlight differences for more detailed study.

To adapt this technique to a given organization requires the establishment of basic functions, activities, and their driving forces. While it may be convenient to establish the functions unilaterally, activities and causes should be determined through a high degree of participation with managers and supervisors. The effectiveness of this approach comes from its simplicity and level of participation.

Structured Brainstorming— Another Use

"What keeps you from being as effective in your job as you would like to be?" This question was posed to the buyers and purchasing agents of a large capital-goods manufacturer who were gathered to brainstorm obstacles to their doing their jobs more effectively. After three hours of brainstorming, over 150 items had been collected. Although many could be classified as gripes, the major portion were substantive. In fact, many had to do with supervisors' and managers' skills. These elements were presented in spite of the fact that those supervisors and managers were participating in the brainstorming session. Brainstorming has been around for quite some time. However, its current highly structured format provides an environment that allows controversial subjects to be discussed in a nonthreatening manner, and develop commitment by the group to the outcome of the sessions.

The process, also known as "nominal group technique," consists of seven sequential steps. We'll use the example of the purchasing department to illustrate each in detail. As noted in Chapter II, the sequential steps are:

1. Purpose Statement

2. Individual Analysis

3. Combined Listing

4. Clarification

5. Evaluation

6. Discussion

7. Selection and Ranking

The problem facing the department was its ability to effectively handle the future workload demands with its existing organization. While there were no significant problems with the current work situation, there was doubt that the new technologies and workloads predicted by the long-range strategic plan could be effectively handled by the group. Some telltale symptoms were beginning to surface that supported these doubts—high turnover, late placement of orders, frequent errors, excessive documentation, and vendor complaints concerning responsiveness. If these conditions continued, the future productivity of the department was doubtful at best. In order to prepare for the future it was necessary to flesh out some of the causes for the current situations.

It was decided that a nominal group session might provide the needed insights into the roots of the difficulties. In order to minimize any perception of threat, a preliminary meeting was held to review the long-range forecasts, the role of the department, the current difficulties, and the plan for a brainstorming session. The buyers, purchasing agents, and supervisors were introduced to the structured approach to brainstorming. It was explained that their perspectives and opinions on how to improve the department's productivity and quality would be sought at a follow-up session.

As is often the case, the session was conducted by a third-party facilitator. This is most desirable when the issues tend to be sensitive because of the objectivity and better control the facilitator can provide. In less sensitive situations, someone from within the organization could be used.

STEP 1—Purpose Statement

The purpose statement sets the tone of the meeting. It must be carefully worded in order to sharpen the group's focus yet not constrain their input or creativity. If the statement is too general, there is a tendency to drift from the subject and to dilute the effort. The participants, carefully selected for their knowledge and involvement in the subject to be treated, met in a conference room equipped with flip charts, markers, tape, and paper and pencils. The room was arranged in a U-shape, to maintain focus on the facilitator and flip charts which were located at the open end of the U. On the flip chart was written the purpose statement:

"WHAT KEEPS YOU FROM BEING AS EFFECTIVE IN YOUR JOB AS YOU WOULD LIKE TO BE"

Phrased in this manner, it does not infer that anyone is ineffective. It does, however, say that people can and want to improve but that there are obstacles. It also hints at the possibility that the roadblocks may be outside their control. And finally, by not using qualifiers on . . . "what keeps you from being as effective, . . . " the door is open to anything and everything.

STEP 2—Individual Analysis

A cardinal rule of employee involvement says, "Nobody knows the job better than the person who does it." A corollary to this might be "Nobody knows the problems better than the people who live with them." Brought together in a nonthreatening environment to look for ways to overcome obstacles, these people will provide a wealth of information. The key, however, is nonthreatening. And this is done by having each participant respond to the purpose statement individually and in writing.

In the case of our purchasing department, the participants were asked to list on the individual pads provided the items and ideas about what keeps them from being effective. By doing this privately, each was encouraged to be honest and creative. This step takes ten to fifteen minutes. The session leader must take care to ensure that nothing disturbs the participants. As each member finishes the assignment, the leader should be alert to side discussions, comments, and other behavior disturbing to the other people. Since this group consisted of three levels of the organization, including direct reports, the lists covered a broad range of concepts that involved almost all the functional areas of the business.

A strength of nominal group processes lies in their ability to overcome "political pressures" found in open, more common meetings containing several organizational levels. Subordinates and superiors want to avoid looking "bad" in the eyes of each other. The first technique employed to avoid this is this individual analysis step. The second technique used comes into play in Step 3—combined listing. In preparing their individual lists, participants should write each idea as concisely as possible—in three to five words. This is important for two reasons: 1) it forces them to think out their ideas completely, and 2) it will be easier to post them on a flip chart in Step 3.

STEP 3—Combined Listing

"I know some of these problems are only bitches, but it sure feels good to say it and see it in writing." This was the observation of one of the buyers in the group as we finished listing each participant's individual contributions. This form of catharsis is a side benefit of the structured-brainstorming process. Most of the other benefits are derived from the design of the process.

After each participant completes the individual analysis sheets, the facilitator must begin the process of combining these lists. Recognizing that each of the group's members prepared their lists privately, the session leader must cause these members to offer their ideas. But this is easier said than done. Most people have attended regular meetings and seen, or been subjected to, the hidden agendas, the politics, the choosing of sides, and perhaps worst of all, the criticism of suggestions or ideas. And because some people feel intimidated by this, they avoid involvement in meetings. Their potential contributions are then lost. To eliminate this situation, the facilitator must maintain discipline and emphasize that during the session criticism is strictly forbidden.

Another important detail to help keep things under control is the way the individuals offer the items on their lists. This is done in rotation, one at a time. This also ensures that everyone has a chance to participate. The mechanics are quite simple:

1. The facilitator asks for someone to voluntarily read one of the items on his or her list—there is usually someone willing to be first. If not, the leader may ask one participant (whoever seems more outgoing than the others) for an item. The item is written on the flip chart for all to see. It may be helpful to have the assistance of someone to act as a scribe to help the facilitator. The scribe should not be a member of the group but should be familiar with the jargon of the group.

2. Each member in rotation then reads only one item from his or her respective lists. These are posted on the flip chart and numbered sequentially starting with one (1).

3. This round-robin continues until someone runs out of contributions to make. He or she should pass. The listings continue skipping any people that want to pass. However, passers are allowed, and should be encouraged, to jump back in when their turns come up again.

4. The facilitator should encourage the group to review the posted items and come up with extensions or combinations of them.

5. After everyone passes, Step 3 ends.

The facilitator must make every effort to draw out input from even the more conservative members of the group. By being courteous, and insistent on no criticism, the leader helps set a nonthreatening contributory environment. The objective should be to maximize the input. Research has shown that many of the better input items come from the last 20% of the combined lists. In fact, when the lists are narrowed down to the best ten, it is not surprising to find that two or three came from the last 20% of the items.*

In the case of the purchasing department, this step identified 152 obstacles that keep workers from being as effective as they would like to be. This is an unusually large amount of data. Normally, one might expect six to eight items per participant. This group generated three to four times as many. Because of the large number of items, the usual clarification process of Step 4 had to be modified to handle this unique situation.

---

*Ira B., Gregerman, *Knowledge Worker Productivity*, AMACOM, A Division of American Management Associations, New York, 1981.

STEP 4—Clarification

The clarification step is designed to ensure that all those present understand the meaning or intent of the items. This is accomplished by reviewing each one and providing the opportunity for questions. However, because of the unusually large quantity, routine treatment would get too complex and cumbersome. Therefore, it was necessary to break down the list into manageable groups before group members could flesh out the key items.

Reviewing the list, the purchasing people found five major categories that could be useful in classifying the 152 items. The following are the categories and the percentage of the total that each contained:

Category	Percent of Total	Quantity
Purchasing department policies and procedures	50	76
Company policies and procedures	11	17
Other departmental requirements	20	30
Combined purchasing and other departments	15	23
Outside of the company	4	6

The categories of course will vary with the data and the circumstances. However, as a guide, the category should relate to the area where the obstacle will likely be addressed or resolved. Now we can look at the list and ask two questions, "Where can the greatest gains be achieved?" and "Where do we get the greatest probability of success?" In this instance, the departmental policies and procedures category was selected for examination. Within this category were opportunities for further subdivisions. This could make the bite-sized pieces even more chewable.

Now given the 76 more manageable items, attention was turned toward clarifying each. First the list was reviewed for obvious duplications or items that were closely related. For example, the "absence of centralized files" was a virtual duplication of "difficult access to files." The group, in reviewing and discussing these two, might decide to eliminate the latter in favor of the former. The second is a symptom of the first. Therefore, if the file location can be resolved, access problems would be cured. Similarly, listing the need for "more clerical help" along with "review clerical functions," and "establish a typing pool," may be combined into one—"review clerical functions."

After weeding these out, the remainder are reviewed by the group one at a time. The question each person must ask himself is, "Do I understand what is meant by the item?" If the answer is negative, the participant is encouraged to ask for an explanation. The facilitator must not allow this step to deteriorate into a sales pitch for the item. Only comments related to its meaning and intent are allowed, not a discourse on benefits or comparisons—that comes later. It would be best if the leader turned the question back to the asker for his or her interpretation. If this fails to illicit a response, volunteers should be sought. After all the items have been reviewed, Step 5 can begin.

Before we get into Step 5, let's review what has been accomplished and what conditions exist. Recall that a major advantage of the structured-brainstorming process is the nonthreatening environment. This has been largely achieved at this point. Individual lists begin the process. Combining and clarifying the lists completes the transformation to anonymity. Experience shows that with few exceptions it is almost impossible at this point to identify a particular listed item with any individual. The rotational process, along with the editing of duplications and similarities, destroys any patterns and reinforces anonymity.

STEP 5—Evaluation

Now that the list has been cut down to manageable quantities, each item must be evaluated for further cuts. The process used in this step is based on the collective judgment of the group expressed by a mathematical-evaluation technique. In this way, the list continues to narrow to the eventual few key productivity-improvement obstacles that the group agrees to work on. Action plans will then be designed to eliminate or overcome the obstacles.

Research has shown that individuals can effectively evaluate and rank up to about ten items from a large list of alternatives. However, the environment must be supportive and nonthreatening. To do this in a group setting demands discipline and confidentiality. The discipline comes from the session leader with confidentiality coming from the secret-ballot voting process. Balloting is done with 3×5 index cards distributed by the facilitator.

With their immediate work areas cleared and the edited list posted in clear view, the participants are asked to independently review the edited list. They are then asked to select those items—equal in number to the index cards they receive—that most effectively respond to the stated purpose of the session. This number is usually between five and eight. In the case of the purchasing department, each person selected the five most important obstacles to productivity improvement. The leader then instructs the group to record their selections on the index cards—one to a card—as follows:

1. In the upper left-hand corner of the card, record the number of the item as it is shown on the posted lists.

2. In the center of the card record the item exactly as it is written on the posted list.

The cards are then spread face up in front of each participant. They are asked to concentrate on the cards and select only the one that they believe responds best to the purpose statement. Having done this, they are asked to place a number, equal to the total number of cards, in the lower right-hand corner of the chosen card. For example, if they were given eight cards to select eight items, the number eight (8) would be used. The normal procedure for ranking a list would now be to go to the next best. But this is not done. Instead, they are next asked to pick the least responsive of the items left before them. This maneuver is used mainly to force a fresh look at the remaining items. When asked initially to pick the best, they will tend to select a descending sequence for the remaining items. However, with the best one now removed from concentration, the remaining items may shift positions. Having now selected the least, it is given a one (1) on the lower right-hand corner of the card. This reversing process continues until all the cards have been numbered. The sequence-selection criteria and numbering pattern for five and eight cards are as follows:

Sequence	Selection Criteria	Five Card Numbering	Eight Card Numbering
1st	Best	5	8
2nd	Least	1	1
3rd	Best	4	7
4th	Least	2	2
5th	Best	3	6
6th	Least		3
7th	Best		5
8th	Least		4

After completing this evaluation and voting process, the cards are collected to tally the votes. The tally is recorded on a flip chart for analysis. Table 4.3 shows what the results would look like for a typical voting process.

Obviously, those items that receive no votes are dropped from the list. Those receiving one or two votes are good candidates for elimination as well. Only items with a large number of votes or a high point tally are retained for continued discussion and final selection and ranking. If the initial list is small, and

TABLE 4.3.
Typical Voting Tally Sheet.

ITEM NUMBER	TALLIES	TOTAL POINTS
1	3,2,3,2,3,1	14
2	2,2,1,1,1,1	8
3	2	2
4	5,4,5,5,5,3,4	31
5	4,4,3	11
6	—	—
7	2,2,1,1,1,1	8
8	—	—
9	1,1	2
10	4,4	8
11	5,5,1,1,1,5,1	19
12	—	—
13	1	1
14	—	—
15	—	—
16	—	—
17	—	—
18	1,1	2
19	5	5
20	—	—
.	.	.
.	.	.
.	.	.
.	.	.
.	.	.
.	.	.
.	.	.
76	1,1,1	3

there is a clear separation of items, the process could end here. However, with a large list, the last two steps should be carried out.

STEP 6—Discussion

The discussion step is an extension of the clarification phase. However, it only focuses on those items that survive the cutting in Step 5. The information in Table 4.3 shows two common phenomena that must be discussed and resolved. First is the conflict between points and total votes. The second is voting polarization. In the first case, items 2, 7, and 10 have the same point count but significantly different plurality. The support for 2 and 7 is broader than for 10 by virtue of the number of votes they received. Therefore, the potential commitment to these two would be broader than for item 10. Since we are trying to build consensus and support for action, 2 and 7 would be preferable to 10. However, that does not preclude considering item 10 at a later date.

The second difficulty is evidenced by substantial polarization in the tally values. Item 11 illustrates this. While all the participants put this item on their list, only three felt it was most important. The other four considered it least important. The reasons for polarization can be different understandings of the items, unequal background information, or divergent judgments. In any case, further discussion seems warranted. The outcome may be a higher point value—ensuring its inclusion in the final selection and ranking process—or a lower value, thus eliminating it.

Again, in the case of the purchasing department, the 76 original productivity-improvement obstacles assigned to departmental policies and procedures had now been narrowed down to 30. However, only the top 20 vote-getters were carried forward to Step 7. Some examples of those were:

- Department secretary should screen all calls.
- Introduction of word-processing equipment.
- Provide more WATTS telephone lines.
- Redistribute commodity assignments.
- Begin a vendor quality-control program.

- Obtain a department-dedicated copy machine.
- Eliminate salesmen's cold calls.
- Standardize quotation and requisition formats.
- Improve office layout to reduce noise and distractions.
- Increase involvement in developing department policies and procedures.

STEP 7—Selection and Ranking

Three methods are commonly used for the final selection and ranking of the surviving items. Each uses a point-rating system but it is applied in different ways. The first two are similar to that described in Step 5. A final rating sheet such as that shown in Figure 4.4 is provided to each participant, who selects a maximum of ten items (less if less than ten items make the final cut). Participants record the item number and description as posted on the flip chart in the space provided. Then, one of two rating approaches are used:

1. A value of one to ten is circled for each item. More than one item can have the same value assigned.

FIGURE 4.4.

Preliminary Evaluation Sheet.

ITEM NO.	DESCRIPTION	VALUATION
_____	_____	1 - 2 - 3 - 4 - 5 - 6 - 7 - 8 - 9 - 10
_____	_____	1 - 2 - 3 - 4 - 5 - 6 - 7 - 8 - 9 - 10
_____	_____	1 - 2 - 3 - 4 - 5 - 6 - 7 - 8 - 9 - 10
_____	_____	1 - 2 - 3 - 4 - 5 - 6 - 7 - 8 - 9 - 10
_____	_____	1 - 2 - 3 - 4 - 5 - 6 - 7 - 8 - 9 - 10
_____	_____	1 - 2 - 3 - 4 - 5 - 6 - 7 - 8 - 9 - 10
_____	_____	1 - 2 - 3 - 4 - 5 - 6 - 7 - 8 - 9 - 10
_____	_____	1 - 2 - 3 - 4 - 5 - 6 - 7 - 8 - 9 - 10
_____	_____	1 - 2 - 3 - 4 - 5 - 6 - 7 - 8 - 9 - 10
_____	_____	1 - 2 - 3 - 4 - 5 - 6 - 7 - 8 - 9 - 10

2. Only one value may be assigned to any item. For example, if an item is given a value of ten, no other can be given a ten. This forces a rank order by each person in the session.

The score sheets are then collected and the values for each item accumulated. The group's preference is then listed in descending point-value order.

The third method uses a forced-pairing evaluation. An evaluation sheet similar to that in Figure 4.5 would be used for ten items. A more complex matrix would be used for twenty final items. Using this format requires that the items be renumbered

FIGURE **4.5.**

Forced-Pairing Evaluation Sheet.

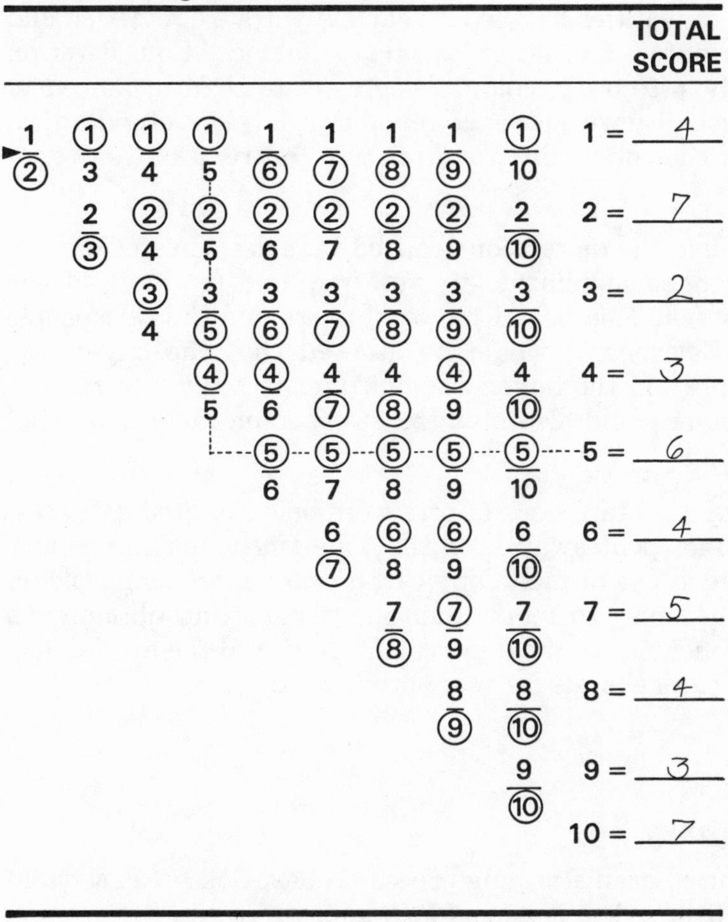

		TOTAL SCORE
	1 =	4
	2 =	7
	3 =	2
	4 =	3
	5 =	6
	6 =	4
	7 =	5
	8 =	4
	9 =	3
	10 =	7

in sequence beginning with one (1), or the alphabet can be used in place of numbers. The original numbers are then dropped.

Paired evaluations are then forced between all possible combinations. Each participant must choose a preferred item from each pair, circling the selected one. For example, between 1 and 2 the choice was 2, between 4 and 5 it was 4, and between 5 and 6,5 was preferred. By adding up the quantity of circled numbers, a total score is obtained. Summing all the participant sheets would then provide a final ordering of items. If a limit is imposed on the number to be dealt with, the highest vote-getters would be preferred.

The finishing touch to this process comes from the development of action plans to overcome the obstacles. In the case of the purchasing department, this resulted in three major changes:

1. The commodities handled by each buyer were reviewed and redistributed for better workload balance. Consideration was given to order volume, degree of negotiations needed, compatibility with other commodities, levels of standardization of the commodity, and relative contribution to overall costs.

2. To reduce the disruptions caused by salesmen's cold calls, prearranged appointments were required for most of the work week. This benefitted the buyers and the salespeople alike. Salespeople would be assured that the buyer was available and the buyer was not unexpectedly interrupted. The buyer could also give the salesperson more undivided attention.

3. The clerical staff work efforts were being diluted by excessive time spent away from the department making copies. Expanded use of multicopy carbon sets, more emphasis on routing copies to more than one person, and obtaining a copy machine for the department increased the availability of the clerical staff for more productive work.

Summary

The structured-brainstorming process is based on seven sequential steps designed to achieve four major objectives:

1. Provide a nonthreatening, creative environment in which a select group can interact to identify productivity-improvement opportunities.

2. Establish a forum conducive to broad participation and the blending of individual perspectives on important productivity-related matters.

3. Make use of a mathematical approach for selecting and rank ordering opportunities to improve productivity.

4. Develop consensus and commitment of the group to the outcome of the brainstorming sessions.

Asking the Right Questions
Nose to Nose

- What keeps you from being as effective as you would like to be?

- What keeps your department or group from working effectively as a unit?

- What do you like about your group that you would like to see persist?

- What changes do you recommend that would make things better for you and your group?

- What things help you do a good job?

- What turns you off about working here?

- How do you know when you are doing a good job?

- What helps you do a good job?

If you could sit down with a few of your managers and ask them these questions, among others, you might be very interested, or shocked, at the replies. Sitting down one on one with managers and supervisors provides a different perspective on the opportunities to improve productivity than would be obtained in a structured-brainstorming session. However, it would not be advisable to attempt so bold a move if you have not been too communicative right along. Secondly, you might not be able to view the data objectively or know how to analyze what you've got. The alternative is to use someone in personnel or training and development within your organization. Another alternative is to hire a consultant. Whichever method is used, confidentiality and objectivity must be maintained. And finally, remember the most important aspect—the development and implementation of action plans to overcome the difficulties uncovered.

These insights, together with information obtained from productivity measures, observations, and informal discussions, provide a comprehensive picture of the organization's productivity status. But, these are only the first steps. All in all, six steps are needed to effectively identify and resolve organization-related problems.

Step 1—Identify problems

Step 2—Gather relative data

Step 3—Analyze the data

Step 4—Develop action plans

Step 5—Implement action plans

Step 6—Evaluate results

While these steps may seem logical—even obvious to some— many managers succumb to the tendency to "jump to cause." Their desire to resolve a problem causes them to jump from problem identification to action-plan development. For a simple problem this may not be too hazardous, but with a complex problem the need to follow the logical steps is more critical. The major reason is to avoid underestimating what is involved in changing the way an organization functions. But, the purpose of this section is to describe a technique for determining productivity-improvement opportunities—especially those perceived by management. The next section on survey techniques will extend this to lower levels of the organization. So let's look at a couple of case studies in which the interview technique was employed.

Case No. 1—Everybody's in Business for Themselves

The company's sales grew tenfold in five years. The spurt was due more to an expansion of the market (fueled by government funding) than from the company's efforts. It was in the right place at the right time. However, the five years that followed were breaking records for being the worst the company had experienced. Margins were falling rapidly, product quality was also suffering, and manufacturing cost overruns were becoming common. The company had expanded its resources to meet the initial demand surge and was reluctant to cut back trained professionals during the leaner period. Management was confident that the situation would reverse, although perhaps not to the former levels. In addition, the professionals—engineers, accountants, programmers, managers—would be needed to solve the difficulties stated above.

While other, more routine actions were being taken, it was decided to discuss the problems with several people from different functions. A series of questions was formulated and interviews were conducted. Anonymity was guaranteed. Some typical responses to "What keeps your department or group from working effectively as a team?" included:

- Poor communications between departments.

- Pressure to watch the budget at the expense of doing the right thing.

- Lack of experienced personnel.

- Unrealistic goals and schedules.

- Too much time trying to keep customers happy.

- Lack of trust by management.

- High turnover of supervisors and managers.

- Insufficient clerical support.

- Department goals mismatching company goals.

Putting this data with other information about the organization, it became apparent that major changes in the management system were necessary. As a result, upper management began to introduce certain changes.

Change	Anticipated Results
Expand middle-management involvement in planning.	• Clearer understanding of goals. • Develop higher trust and mutual respect.
Provide extensive management-development training.	• Increased managerial skills and lower turnover. • Improved interfunctional cooperation.
Initiate work-flow analysis programs.	• Better distribution of project assignments. • Improved paperwork flow and usage. • Lowered demand on nonessential clerical time.
Focus customer service in one function.	• More responsiveness to customer complaints. • More complete information for problem solving. • Reduced interference and impact on functional departments.

Case No. 2—Separation Doesn't Make the Heart Grow Fonder

Designing and manufacturing sophisticated capital equipment is complicated enough, but when these two functions are a continent apart the complexities increase geometrically. Historically, the company has grown—but not spectacularly. Profits, margins, and sales have kept pace with the industry and inflation. Labor relations in the manufacturing plants have been very good, but this was normal for the industry as a whole. With the number of orders declining, tight controls had to be instituted to contain rising costs. The president of the company was concerned with several recent trends:

- There was a drop in the open support of the company's goals.

- Decisions were being kicked upstairs with increasing frequency.

- Project-installation schedules were slipping.

- Design problems were appearing more frequently.

- The field personnel were showing signs of unrest.

Since the bulk of problems appeared to occur with the field-service and installation personnel, attention was focused there. The manager of that function took over the department about 18 months prior to recognition of the trends. There was a strong suspicion that the autocratic management style of the new manager was a contributing cause to the problems. To evaluate this, subordinates were interviewed with the knowledge and agreement of the manager. Again, confidentiality was assured the individuals. The manager was given the feedback, and no details were provided the president.

Of the several questions asked, two elicited the most interesting responses. The first, "What things get in the way of your doing a good job?" generated the following typical responses:

- Not being told I do a good job.

- Lack of clear guidelines.

- Too much interference in decision making.

- No recognition for accomplishments.

- Excessive nit-picking.

- Constant finger-pointing.

- Job assignments not matching personal goals.

The second question was, "What turns you off about working here?" The responses included:

- The boss criticizes you behind your back.

- No recognition for doing a good job.

- I don't get the backup I need.

- No one seems to have an honest interest in my opinion.

- Not enough openness and mutual respect.

- Not knowing where you stand.

One individual summed it up best of all. "Most companies function by delegation of authority," he said. "This one operates by delegation of *blame.*"

When the data were reviewed with the department manager, she commented, "That's about the same responses that I got a few years ago when I ran another group." It was obvious that she was content with her style, and so was her boss—at least up to this point. The prognosis for the situation in this department was not encouraging. Other managers took a more enlightened view of data eventually collected in their areas.

Introducing Change

When using the interview approach to assessing opportunities to improve productivity, the manager must be aware that he or she is instituting a change process. In so doing, the manager must be willing to follow through with actions. If not, the excitement of elevated expectations can be turned into frustration and resistance to future efforts at improvement, or even worse, into mistrust for the organization. To successfully implement changes requires the answers to three questions:

1. Why should the individual change?
2. What's in it for me?
3. What is the practicality of the change process?

In the first question, the answers should deal with an identifiable "need." The second requires some form of payback or "benefit" to the manager. The last question focuses on the issues of how the change will be introduced—specifically the level of "involvement" of those employees who are the targets for change. The relationship between "needs," "benefits," and "involvement" determine the probability for a successful change process to occur. It can be expressed mathematically as:

$$\text{Successful Change Probability} = \text{Need} \times \text{Benefits} \times \text{Involvement}$$

The important characteristic of this relationship is that success depends on the multiplicative effects of needs, benefits, and involvement. Consider that if any of these were zero—no need, or no benefit, or no involvement—the probability of success would be zero. Similarly, if any of these were very small, the probability of success would also be very small. Think about some of your own experiences from this perspective and you may discover why there was so much trouble getting change to happen or why the change failed to take hold. Two examples will help illustrate these relationships.

In the first, the manager of a large technology-oriented organization is dissatisfied with the lack of cooperation and interdependence of those reporting directly to him. Virtually all disputes are delegated upward. Too much of his time was being diverted from more critical issues. With a general idea of the potential gains and benefits, but no practical approach at his disposal, attempts to change this situation were unsuccessful. To remedy this, internal consultants were used. Involving department personnel in meetings and interviews to discuss the problems, action plans were developed to increase the level of communications and teamwork and provide management training and development.

The results included improved organizational effectiveness by increasing decision making at lower organizational levels. What's more, the department manager could now devote more time to the business problems that were still there.

In another situation, the manager of a staff function was well satisfied with the existing organization's short-term capabilities. There was, however, uncertainty about its ability to identify and act on the obstacles to achieving clearly defined long-range goals. Using the achievement of these goals as the driving force, participative problem-solving teams were formed. They identified major obstacles and developed action plans to reduce or eliminate their effects. The results were a higher chance of meeting the long-range goals through a greater sense of ownership, improved teamwork, and higher department productivity.

Survey and Questionnaire Routes to Opportunities

Surveys and questionnaires come in all forms and sizes, from one-page checksheets to 100-plus question booklets, from simple "yes" or "no" responses to the selection of one of several statements that clarify a position. Whichever is used, it is imperative that feedback be provided to those participating and that there be a sincere attempt to resolve problems that are identified—especially when the results seem to be contrary to what you might have expected or hoped for. Executives have been known to be surprised that their subordinates viewed conditions quite differently than they did. In this section we will look at three different approaches and uses for the written survey.

To Determine Training and Development Needs

Very few people would disagree that employee training and development is a necessity. However, you get a lot of argument concerning the specific areas of need. Recent research on supervisory training found that the most common subjects covered in off-the-job training dealt with motivation, employee development, communications, leadership, and human relations.* Other subjects lagged considerably behind. To find out what your own people need you should ask them.

Figure 4.6 shows a simple checksheet of training areas. The numbers are used to measure the degree of need. The two-col-

FIGURE 4.6.
Survey of Skill-Training Needs.

SKILL AREA	YES	FOR ME UNSURE		NO	YES	FOR MY SUBORDINATES UNSURE		NO
Time Management	5	4 3	2	1	5	4 3	2	1
Holding Effective Meetings	5	4 3	2	1	5	4 3	2	1
Team Building	5	4 3	2	1	5	4 3	2	1
Performance Appraisal	5	4 3	2	1	5	4 3	2	1
Effective Communications	5	4 3	2	1	5	4 3	2	1
General Management Skills	5	4 3	2	1	5	4 3	2	1
Subordinate Development	5	4 3	2	1	5	4 3	2	1
Understanding Motivation	5	4 3	2	1	5	4 3	2	1
Leadership Skills	5	4 3	2	1	5	4 3	2	1
Introducing Change	5	4 3	2	1	5	4 3	2	1
Budgeting	5	4 3	2	1	5	4 3	2	1
Setting Goals	5	4 3	2	1	5	4 3	2	1
Human Relations	5	4 3	2	1	5	4 3	2	1
Problem Solving	5	4 3	2	1	5	4 3	2	1
Planning and Organizing	5	4 3	2	1	5	4 3	2	1
Career Path Development	5	4 3	2	1	5	4 3	2	1
_____	5	4 3	2	1	5	4 3	2	1
_____	5	4 3	2	1	5	4 3	2	1
_____	5	4 3	2	1	5	4 3	2	1

COMMENTS:

*K. Culbertson and M. Thompson, "An Analysis of Supervisory Training Needs," *Training & Development Journal*, February 1980, p. 58.

umn format is intended to be used by the manager to assess his or her needs as well as those of his or her subordinates. All the other people would fill in the "for me" column, or a separate single-column format could be used. This little survey was given to a vice president of engineering and his immediate subordinates. The relative position of the skills needed most, from the perspective of the managers, was out of phase with their boss. The results are shown next.

With a few exceptions, the lists are polarized. The vice president believes his people need basic skill development. The managers do not feel these are nearly as important as budgeting, meeting, and team-building skills. Both agree on the low level of need for further training in performance appraisal and problem solving. This last situation was expected, considering the company's excellent performance-appraisal process and the inherent problem-solving skills of engineers.

Vice President	Managers
1. General management skills	1. Budgeting
2. Leadership skills	2. Holding effective meetings
3. Understanding motivation	3. Team building
4. Time management	4. Time management
5. Budgeting	5. Setting goals
6. Planning and organizing	6. Planning and organizing
7. Effective communications	7. Subordinate development
8. Setting goals	8. Career-path development
9. Holding effective meetings	9. Introducing change
10. Human relations	10. Effective communications
11. Career-path development	11. General management skills
12. Subordinate development	12. Leadership
13. Team building	13. Understanding motivation
14. Introducing change	14. Human relations
15. Performance appraisal	15. Performance appraisal
16. Problem solving	16. Problem solving

Which list is closer to actuality can be determined only by further investigation and analysis. As was the situation here, the VP's list was closer to the truth than was the subordinates. Many of the high level items on their lists were the VP's hot buttons. The outcome was the introduction of a management-skills development program with customized add-on modules in budgeting and group dynamics.

To Determine Attitudes and Climate

As the manager of an organization producing a product or service, what would you assess the attitudes of your employees toward their jobs, supervisors, the company? If they are not positive, productivity can be substantially lower than desired. The management process itself will have impact on attitudes at all levels and establish the climate of the organization. You can get a good feel for this by reading the following questions and circling the appropriate answer (? = not sure).

1. Information is exchanged between all organizational levels through a regular communications program.   YES   ?   NO
2. The company provides supervisory training programs for experienced and new supervisors.   YES   ?   NO
3. The wage and benefits structure is competitive with similar jobs in the industry and area.   YES   ?   NO
4. Employees are encouraged to provide ideas concerning safety, working conditions, productivity improvements, and other job or company-related matters.   YES   ?   NO
5. Employees receive frequent updates on the company's performance in the market place, new products, and changes of interest to them.   YES   ?   NO
6. There is a comprehensive performance-appraisal system in place and used regularly.   YES   ?   NO
7. In general, subordinates are involved in decisions that affect them and their work group.   YES   ?   NO

8. Middle and first-level managers meet
   regularly with subordinates to discuss
   upper-management decisions.   YES   ?   NO

If you answered *YES* to all the statements, you have an unusual organization. More likely, though, you have a majority
of question marks and even a few *NOs*. The negatives and un-
knowns then become targets for further investigation and improvement. Obviously, these questions dealt with broad general areas. But they do give you a feel for conditions as "you"
see them. What about the others in your organization? How
do they see things? Do your responses represent the way
things are or as you wish them to be? To find out, you need
more questions and input from every level of the organization.
The format should provide feedback to you and the other managers and supervisors, concerning how your actions and behavior affect the subordinates.

The feedback approach has one major problem. Not all managers will be receptive or responsive to the opinions and attitudes of their subordinates. Feedback is a form of performance
appraisal in reverse. Because this process demands some self-
evaluation and soul searching, managers may attack the validity
of the data rather than change their methods. On the other hand,
many managers would welcome the opportunity to identify and
improve weaknesses—provided a method is available.

The other element of feedback is related to those that provide the data—the employees at large. Most of the better survey
instruments provide the opportunity to evaluate areas beyond
the leader-subordinate interactions—areas such as wage, salary,
and benefit administration, quality of work life, and organizational structure. However, before anyone embarks on a survey,
some of the advantages and disadvantages should be noted and
understood (Figure 4.7). In the vast majority of cases, survey design, administration, and analysis should be left to experienced
consultants.

A Word or Two About Surveys

As you might expect, numerous surveys are available, both stan-
dardized and customized. However, on a purely cost basis, the
standard instruments are preferred. The problem is deciding

FIGURE 4.7.

Employee Attitude and Climate Surveys.

ADVANTAGES	DISADVANTAGES
• Provides a broad perspective of organizational climate on many factors.	• Results can be biased if the sample size used is not representative.
• Anonymity will encourage frankness.	• A long survey can cause tedium and questionable data for the closing questions.
• Standardized surveys are less expensive than customized ones.	• Customized surveys are expensive.
• Focuses on problems that affect organizational functioning.	• Employee expectations can be elevated beyond management's planned level of action.
• Monitors the effects of organizational and business changes.	• Standardized surveys usually do not cover specialized areas of interest.
• Can be used to compare different functional managers within the organization.	• Broad-based norms for comparison will not be available for customized surveys.
• Helps to determine management strengths and weaknesses for long-range planning.	

which one to use. The Center for Creative Leadership offers some guidelines to consider in making the selection.*

1. The survey format should be consistent—the layout of the questions and scoring pattern should not change. For example, if the first statement required a response of 1 to 5 for "always agree" to "always disagree," all the questions should be in that pattern. If some response patterns are reversed, there may be serious doubts about the validity of that particular data.

2. Provide for open-ended comments. Some respondents may feel the need to go beyond just circling a number or coloring in a space. Responses can also provide insight about more specific problems. Open-ended questions may also create the

---

*A. M. Morrison, M. W. McCall, and D. L. DeVries, *Feedback to Managers: A Comprehensive Review of Twenty-Four Instruments,* Technical Report No. 8, Center for Creative Leadership, Greensboro, NC, 1978.

aura of individualization. Concerns over identification of the writer are usually groundless. No one but the consultant sees the actual survey instrument. The client is given a typed transcription of the responses.

3. At least five statements should be used for each dimension in order to assure reliability of the responses for any given dimension—delegation, control, group interaction. This is needed to provide a look at any given dimension from different perspectives.

4. Provide a picture of how far change has to go. Most surveys deal only with the current situation. A few provide respondents the opportunity to indicate where they would like the situation to be, for example, "To what degree does your supervisor delegate responsibility?" and "To what degree would you like responsibility delegated?" The gap between the *current* and the *like to be* is an indication of the magnitude of the change desired.

5. The survey should be consistent over time. In order to track changes in climate over long periods of time, the questionnaire should remain unchanged over the period being evaluated.

6. Involve top management in the survey and feedback process. This is vital in order to establish credibility and commitment to improvements.

7. Feedback to managers must be kept confidential. Respondent anonymity and individual managerial feedback reports must be kept confidential. It is important to emphasize this during the administration of the survey to encourage honest input and positive responses by the managers.

Tying the Audit to Results— A Case Study

"Thank God I got through another day."
"You got to watch the b_____ds every minute."

These were representative comments of the hourly worker's and manager's feelings of this unionized midwestern operation of a large corporation, according to the senior manager responsible for turning it around. And turn around it did—from the lowest productivity operation in the company, if not the industry, to one of the best. But it took nearly five years of dedicated effort.

The effort involved over 10,000 hours of interviews and discussions with a cross-section of all the employees including managers. All levels, functions, and job categories were included like a diagonal slice through the organization to examine its innermost working relationships. They found several common threads running through the entire operation.

- No sense of pride or loyalty to the company or its products.

- Apathetic management toward employee problems and concerns.

- Lack of appreciation for the efforts of employees and cynicism when it was offered.

- Mutual suspicion rather than mutual respect between workers and supervisors.

- Acceptance of poor or below standard workmanship.

- Management pressing for unrealistic goals.

- Little or no involvement of employees in decisions.

- Unresolved union grievances and frequent walk-outs.

To overcome this situation, a comprehensive plan was developed and implemented. Training programs in communications were begun. An MBO process was introduced at all levels, including hourly. And a labor-management committee was started to resolve job problems and expand employee involvement. The emphasis in all the programs was on identifying and discussing job-related problems and barriers that prevented the workers from doing their jobs.

Hourly workers, supervisors, and managers began to understand one another better. Through this understanding, respect for each others' jobs and job pressures began to emerge. But all was not smooth. Many old-line managers found it very hard to accept criticism, admit they had made mistakes, and commit to and attempt to change. Some managers never made it, but so too didn't some union leaders. They refused to take part in the programs or even support them. It is suspected that they may have looked on this effort as a union-busting move by the company.

After the employees had completed the training program, a climate survey was conducted among the nonmanagement employees. Fourteen dimensions were measured. Table 4.4 shows the results of the survey in 1977, at the completion of the training, and in 1978, after a year of trying out the newfound skills. The data are presented as a percentage of surveyed employees that looked favorably on the company's performance in each area measured. In all but three cases (nos. 4, 11, 14) significant improvement was found. Of the three, some improvement, although small, was seen in the area of respect (no. 11)—which was already high in 1977. What is most dramatic, though, is not the

TABLE **4.4.**
Employee Attitude and Climate Survey Results.

	PERCENT NONMANAGEMENT PERSONNEL WHO SAID COMPANY PERFORMANCE WAS FAVORABLE	
	1977	**1978**
1. Ideas and suggestions were sought	43	54
2. Supervisor keeps me appraised on my performance	52	59
3. The company is open and honest in dealing with employees	19	27
4. Prompt action is taken on suggestions and complaints	49	48
5. Supervisor keeps me informed about changes that may affect my job	50	58
6. The overall morale of employees is good	23	33
7. There are opportunities for advancement	23	36
8. I have open communications with my supervisor	81	89
9. There are open communications with management above my supervisor	31	48
10. The general communications between management and nonmanagement employees is good	60	78
11. I am treated with respect as an individual	67	71
12. Management is concerned with employees' interests and needs	42	56
13. I am satisfied with the information received regarding top-level policy decisions	12	20
14. My job is interesting and challenging	68	68

values themselves but the changes that occurred over the year's time. Increases as high as 67% for information regarding top-level policy decisions were found (no. 13).

The bottom line after several years of effort was a $10.2 million savings in labor costs in 1978 alone. But no layoffs were allowed. The reductions would come from transfers and normal attrition. The measurements showed the following improvements:

PRODUCTIVITY	1977	1978	Hours	Dollars
Production (units/hour)	9.76	12.01	236,100	$5,200,000
Maintenance (units/hour)	5.46	6.70	154,500	2,800,000
Services (units/hour)	4.89	6.74	128,900	2,200,000
			519,000	$10,200,000
SAFETY				
Injuries/100 employees/year	5.44	3.65		
Preventable accidents	70	52		
SERVICE				
Missed appointments	2.40%	2.16%		
Customer complaints per week	4.57	4.53		

The small improvement in customer complaints speaks loudly of the cause and effect lag between product quality and customer dissatisfaction. It is easy and quick to develop dissatisfied customers. To win them back is a long, hard struggle especially if some lower-quality products are still floating around. The savings were so dramatic that other units of the company have adapted the strategies and techniques.

Beginning With Your Own Organization

Frequently, the best place to look for improvements is within one's own organization. And the search should start with those factors that management can do something about. Some will be easy; some will require small adjustments; and some will require major changes in operations. For example, a large national engineering company was searching for opportunities to lower costs and increase productivity. One of the areas of investigation was the huge number of copies made each year. The total number, over 6,000,000 in all, if stacked one on top of another, would be over 1500 feet high, more than 4.3 times the height of the building that produced them. With that kind of volume, even small changes add up to big dollars.

Many factors in organizational life affect the overall climate. The climate in turn influences the levels of productivity, costs, turnover, safety, quality, and many others. Some of management's controllable factors include:

- Clearly defined and communicated objectives.
- Participative management styles.
- Effective communications.
- Application of state-of-the-art technology.
- A minimum of controls, policies, and procedures.
- Training of managers, supervisors, and workers.

To help evaluate your organization's status on these and other factors, a short survey is presented in Figure 4.8. To complete the survey, read each statement and place an *X* in the appropriate column: common practice, frequently, infrequently, almost never, and not sure. When you have finished, look at those statements marked infrequently, almost never, and not sure. These areas provide opportunities for improvement and should be tackled first. It is always best to get your own house in order before entering into someone else's.

Summary

The process of auditing the organization for productivity-improvement opportunities is an important element in the overall process of improvement. While we have looked at only four techniques—measurement, structured brainstorming, one-on-one interviewing, and climate surveys—virtually anything that high-

FIGURE 4.8.

A Survey of Organizational Productivity.

	Common Practice	Frequent	Not Sure	Infrequently	Almost Never
1. Accomplishments are adequately recognized.					
2. Business objectives, problems, and performance are reviewed with employees on a regular basis.					
3. Functional groups interact effectively and are supportive of one another.					
4. Productivity levels and improvements are measured and communicated to all organizational levels.					
5. The organization is sensitive and responsive to employees' concerns, frustrations, and needs.					
6. Controls are minimal and encourage flexibility and innovation.					
7. Portions of capital budgets are used to maintain state-of-the-art technology.					
8. Job performance and expectations are clearly and consistently communicated.					
9. Innovation and challenge of the status quo is encouraged, acknowledged, and rewarded when successful.					
10. The management group is involved in the design and implementation of major changes or new policies and procedures.					
11. Training and development opportunities are available for management and nonmanagement personnel.					
12. There is effective interfacing between the company functions and the customer.					
13. Managers prepare annual productivity-improvement plans and review progress periodically.					
14. Accountability for assigned responsibilities is clearly communicated and understood.					
15. The organization is dedicated to excellence in its people and its products.					
16. Projects and product-development activities are pertinent to, and supportive of, the organization's overall objectives.					

lights potential improvements may be used. Look into turnover and absenteeism statistics, budget performance, customer complaints, exit interview reports, inventory shortages and stockouts, recruiting difficulties, quality control reports, percentage of complaints or grievances, that don't get resolved quickly, and dozens of other possibilities. Most, if not all, of this data should be readily available or easy to obtain from existing reports. Once the opportunities are found, changes must occur. It is at this stage that many improvement efforts fail.

Change is accomplished when there is a need for it, when benefits will result, and when those impacted by the change are involved in its implementation. Even these conditions will not be sufficient if management itself has not prepared properly for the changes. This usually requires a loosening of the reins, more accessibility, sharing of information, more involvement in decision making, and increased exposure to criticism. Not only will these things help to put over the changes, but they will also go a long way toward ensuring its permanence.

CHAPTER **5**

Xxactly!

THIS TYPXWRITXR is xxcxllxnt xxcxpt for onx kxy. Thx 25 othxr lxttxrs work finx, but just onx goof-off lousxs up thx wholx job.

Amxrica has thx samx problxm. Wx arx dxfinitxly in a production compxtition with othxr nations. Output pxr man is what makxs a favorablx balancx of tradx and holds down inflation. In thx othxr lxading industrial nations productivity growth pxr man is rising dramatically. Our own has lxvxlxd out at around 0.3 pxrcxnt. Thxrx arx sxvxral rxasons, but onx is thx plain fact that onx in xvxry crowd of us has quit putting out.

In any dxpartmxnt of 27 pxoplx, if onx kxy pxrson goofs off or goofs up, it lousxs up thx output just about this bad.

In a work forcx of about 102 million pxoplx, onx out of 26 adds up to ovxr 3,949,000 gold brickxrs or goof-offs, which is xnough to jinx up thx wholx country.

—William D. Xllis

Putting It All Together

At this point in our discussion of productivity improvement, we have covered the basic national situations, methods of measuring productivity at various organizational levels, the benefits and techniques of involving employees in productivity improvement, and methods for determining the opportunities for improvement. The objective of Chapter 5 is to gather these concepts into a logical *pattern* of events so we have a model that can be a foundation for continued improvement. You may have noted that we are not talking about a *sequence* of events. This is intentional. A sequence requires a chronological order of events. The reader will likely have some of the elements of the model already in place. It is important that you build on what you have before adding anything. For example, a steering committee is highly recommended for a broad-based productivity-improvement strategy. The makeup of this committee is similar to that of a quality circle's steering committee. Investigate combining both functions before starting a new committee. The same may apply to committees in Scanlon plans.

Figure 5.1 shows the model as it is currently being used by large and small companies. To facilitate implementation, the elements of the model are grouped into six phases.

Phase I.   Commitment and Organization

Phase II.   Planning, Measurement, and Awareness

Phase III.   Opportunity Assessment and Goals

Phase IV.   Managerial and Supervisory Involvement

Phase V.   Selection and Implementation of Techniques

Phase VI.   Rewards and Recognition and Feedback

FIGURE 5.1

A Productivity-Improvement Model.

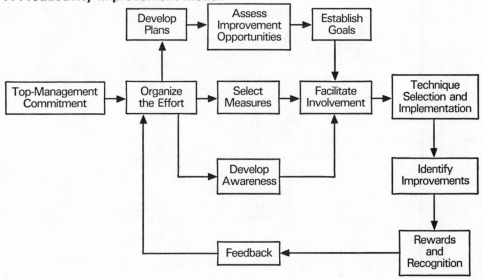

© Ira B. Gregerman, 1981

To see how these phases fit together chronologically, look at Figure 5.2. This is a milestone chart for a smaller New England company (sales less than $100 million). From the start of the process in January, 1982, it takes between five and six months to implement the first technique at trial locations in a plant and office area. It will take an additional two to three months to begin seeing results. By contrast, a large New England company (sales over $3 billion) using the same model has a milestone chart twice as long though not any more complex. The time frame depends more on the communications and approval channels than anything else. Be that as it may, the model is flexible enough to fit both extremes. Perhaps just as important, it will also be suitable for small organizational subunits of a major corporate entity.

This chapter then, will detail some of the model's elements that have not been covered so far. Specifically, we will look at top-management commitment, organizing and managing the strategy, developing awareness, planning the process, selecting test sites for technique evaluation, rewards and recognition and feedback. The other blocks have been adequately treated else-

FIGURE 5.2.
Milestone Chart—Productivity-Improvement Model.

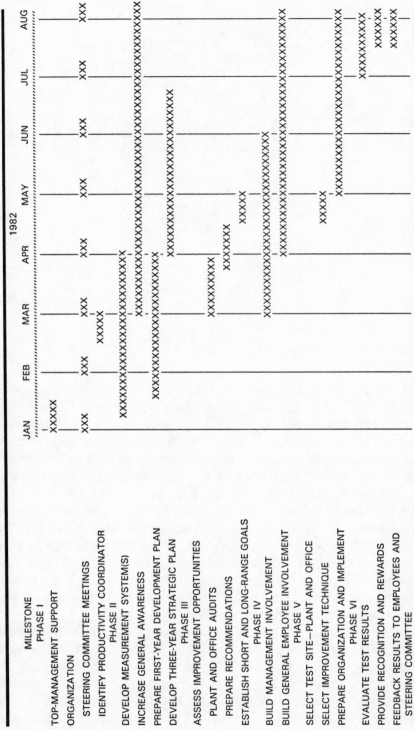

where. And lastly, the final chapter provides resources and a comprehensive bibliography for research, education, and just digging deeper into the subject of productivity.

Top-Management Commitment

Providing money will not guarantee the success of a productivity effort. To be successful, the top management of the organization must become involved in the planning and goal-setting functions. The company must insist that productivity be incorporated into the company's routine business and budget-planning cycles as well as the MBO program. To succeed over the long run, top management must work toward making productivity an everyday thing. And this usually means change. If the leadership of the organization sets the example and follows through, you are off to a good start. Here are a few things to consider:

- Hold regular meetings with employees to discuss current business conditions.

- Encourage questions and give frank answers. If you don't know an answer, say so. Then find the answer and feed it back at the next meeting or through the company publications.

- Integrate productivity into operational and financial planning.

- Build productivity achievements into the performance-appraisal system.

- Participate in improvement activities—award presentations, productivity seminars, other presentations—as often as practical.

- Use the results of improvement efforts in a positive way. Avoid punitive use of results that may fall short of goals.

- Ensure an ongoing dialogue among all levels of the company.

Avoid using memos and proclamations as a sole way of demonstrating commitment. Employees who do not *see* top management may perceive this as a strategic weakness or lack of commitment. It's a little like the cartoon showing a factory worker in front of a large bulletin board reading the latest management-time edict, "Effective January 1, all employees will be motivated."

Invariably, the question of the cost of commitment is raised. While it is impossible to give an exact dollar figure, there is a way to estimate the number of people in your organization who would be involved in the first year start up. Based on data from several major corporations with productivity-improvement efforts, the author has developed a graphical method to determine the number of full-time equivalent personnel that would be involved with a company-wide program. Figure 5.3 shows the relationship between sales per employee and the total equivalent full-time people expressed as a percent of the total number of employees. This is how the graph would work for a company with 1,800 employees and $200,000 in sales per employee.

1. Draw a line from 200,000 on the vertical axis, horizontally so that it intersects the two diagonal lines.

2. At these points of intersection, draw a vertical line down to the horizontal axis.

3. Read the corresponding percentages, 0.35% for a low and 0.53% for a high estimate.

4. Multiply these percentages by the total employment to give an estimate of between 6 and 9 full-time equivalent employees. What this says is that if we added all the part-time effort (accounting, data processing, training, manufacturing) to any full-time people (plant level productivity managers), the total would be between 6 and 9 people.

Here are the results of three different companies using this method.

Industry	Sales (Revenue) per Employee	Total Employees	Equivalent Full-time Employees Involved
Capital Equipment	$128,000	1,200	3 to 4
Utility	$155,000	3,900	11 to 16
Banking	$110,000	15,000	32 to 47

FIGURE 5.3.

Estimating the Number of Employees Involved in a Productivity-Im-provement Effort.

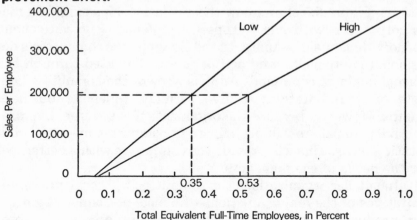

Total Equivalent Full-Time Employees, in Percent

© Ira B. Gregerman, Holden, MA, 1982.

It must be emphasized that this is an estimate of the first year's extent of commitment of in-house personnel. Additional costs for consultants would have to be factored in.

Organizing the Effort

To carry forward the productivity-improvement commitment and to provide ongoing guidance and resources, some degree of formalized structure should be provided. Generally, this takes on the form of a steering committee and a productivity manager. The establishment of a committee and the identification of the manager are another sign of top-management commitment. The steering committee is very important to the long-term success of the effort. It is a working committee. It is not, as some would say, a group of the *unfit* appointed by the *unwilling* to do the *unnecessary*.

The two organizational elements are linked. The manger is a member of the steering committee. In some cases the manager may be the chairperson. The steering committee is charged with the responsibility of ensuring that the productivity effort has all the resources needed to succeed. It interacts with all the elements of the model (Figure 5.4). In organizations large enough to have several productivity managers, the committee can provide a coordination and communications linkage between remote locations. Figure 5.5 shows how these relationships exist in a major corporation with over 100 operating plants assigned to about 30 individual business units. In the example, the committee's decisions, requirements, and activities are channeled through the normal chain of command. As it is shown, the committee consists of representatives of five permanent-member business groups. However, because the organization is so large, five productivity managers will participate in committee meetings on a rotating basis. This will provide the committee with a better feel for the needs of the managers.

In smaller organizations the committee will consist of representatives of the major functions—finance, personnel, engineering, production, sales and marketing, among others. The committee size should be limited to about 8–10 people. If the committee is smaller, important perceptions and inputs could be missed. If larger, meetings can become cumbersome and lack de-

FIGURE 5.4.

The Productivity-Improvement Steering Committee Functions.

FIGURE 5.5.

The Steering Committee Maintains Line-Organization Communications.

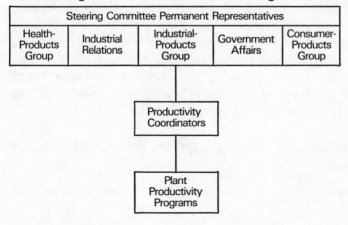

cisiveness. The role of the steering committee includes the following elements:

- Advise and guide productivity-improvement strategies.

- Establish company (or plant) and functionally specific productivity-improvement objectives.

- Develop long-range strategic productivity objectives.

- Provide continuous emphasis and commitment to the effort.

- Evaluate and provide for the needs of the productivity coordinators.

- Establish reporting procedures.

- Assess potential productivity-improvement opportunities.

- Maintain awareness of the productivity impact of factors external to the organization.

- Coordinate the selection of productivity-measurement systems and improvement techniques.

- Monitor the impact of company policies on productivity.

The placement and title of the productivity manager's job ranges from a coordinator, at an operating plant, to a corporate vice president, such as is found in TRW and Westinghouse. And as you might expect, compensation will also vary. Typically, in

1980, total compensation averaged $34,300 at the plant level to an average of $97,000 at the corporate level.* Productivity managers generally function alone as a staff person. Some, however, do have small staffs averaging about four people. John Grahn, General Mills' Director of Corporate Productivity Improvement, noted that "A productivity manager is successful when they go from the *anonymous* to the *misunderstood.*"† To break from anonymity, the productivity manager's role—whatever the title or placement—takes on several characteristics:

- Actively pursue productivity improvements at all levels of the organization.

- Assess and act, or cause action, on improvement opportunities.

- Develop and submit improvement plans to the steering committee.

- Assist in selecting and implementing improvement techniques.

- Coordinate activities with local and corporate employee-relations personnel.

- Recommend changes to corporate policies that may interfere with productivity-improvement efforts.

- Coordinate and report on improvement-project results.

- Maintain awareness of external political and technological events of interest to the organization.

- Build broad-based support for the improvement activities.

Chapter VI contains job descriptions for four different organizations with productivity managers. They are intended as a guide only. It is best to develop your own. Also in Chapter VI is a list of organizations and companies that have an emphasis on productivity and/or quality of work life. It would be wise for the newly appointed productivity manager to become familiar with one or more of them.

---

*Unpublished survey of the American Productivity Management Association Membership, APMA, Skokie, IL, Sept. 1980.
†APMA Fall Conference, St. Louis, MO, Sept. 23, 1981.

Planning for Productivity Improvement

It is beyond the scope of this book to educate the reader on the fine points of planning. Where possible, productivity planning should be integrated into the routine business and budget-planning cycles. What we will look at is a way of evaluating which department, or plant, you might want to begin with in your productivity effort, or where to test a technique.

Figure 5.6 contains fifteen criteria to be considered in selecting a test site. The pertinent questions are intended to help the productivity manager evaluate each dimension. A point value of from 1 to 5 is assigned depending on whether it is unacceptable, poor, fair, good, or excellent. Then sum the points for each prospective test site using the form in Figure 5.7.

A site that scores less than 35 points should be avoided. A score of 60 or better is an excellent prospect and should be used. Between 36 and 59 points is undecisive. However, if no site scores over 60, a high midspan score of 45 or better would be preferred over a score of 39 to 45. These are, of course, only guides. You may want to weight each of the criteria or develop ones of your own. In any case, it provides a checklist of characteristics to consider.

Some key tactical considerations to be incorporated in a productivity-planning process should include:

- Realistic short-term expectations built into the long-range plan.

- Establish workable definitions of productivity for the various functions.

- Productivity plans must support the general business plan.

- An understanding that it is the functional manager's explicit responsibility for improvement.

- Plans to build on the organization's historical strengths.

- Assurance that individual projects are mutually supportive.

FIGURE 5.6.

Productivity Improvement—Test-Site Evaluation Criteria.

CRITERIA	PERTINENT QUESTIONS
1. Worker Receptivity	What is the anticipated level of acceptance of nonmanagement personnel to productivity-improvement techniques?
2. Management Receptivity	What is the anticipated level of acceptance of the management personnel to the concepts of productivity-improvement techniques? What are the anticipated benefits to the test site?
3. Size Manageability	Is the test site size controllable by available management resources? Can the test program be conducted within test site objectives?
4. Test Management Compatability	What is the anticipated level of cooperation between the test-site management and the implementation personnel?
5. Test-Site Validity	Is the proposed test site representative of other company sites?
6. Success Measurability	Can the tests be objectively evaluated and measured with existing measurement systems?
7. Cost:Benefit Relativity	What are the potential benefits vs. costs of the technique to the test site?
8. Resource Availability	What is the level of resource commitment to the test program (manpower, budget, materials)?
9. Time-Benefit Relativity	What is the relationship between potential benefits and the time to complete the test?
10. Success Probability	What is the probability of the tests to be successful and show demonstrable results?
11. Financial Stability	Is the test-site financial position profitable and stable (sales, margins, inventory)?
12. Management Stability	What is the probability that the management of the site will be stable through the test?
13. Complexity of the Trial Technique	Will the test technique be kept simple enough not to require extraordinary commitment?
14. Site Visibility	Is the test site highly visible to upper management in order to enhance credibility?
15. Testing Personnel Capability	What is the credibility of the test implementation personnel relative to the technique?

© Ira B. Gregerman, 1981.

FIGURE 5.7.

Productivity Improvement Test-Site Criteria Evaluation Form.

TEST SITE CRITERIA	SITE A	SITE B	SITE C	SITE D
1. Worker Receptivity				
2. Management Receptivity				
3. Size Manageability				
4. Management Compatibility				
5. Test-Site Validity				
6. Success Measurability				
7. Cost:Benefit Relativity				
8. Resource Availability				
9. Time-Benefit Relativity				
10. Success Probability				
11. Financial Stability				
12. Management Stability				
13. Complexity of Program				
14. Site Visibility				
15. Testing Personnel				
TOTAL SCORE				

Assign a point value of 1, 2, 3, 4, or 5 to coincide with your evaluation of unacceptable, poor, fair, good, or excellent to each criterion.
© Ira B. Gregerman, 1981.

Developing Awareness

It is important that all employees become aware of the purpose and benefits associated with increased productivity. Further, awareness may be necessary in order to put to rest any misgivings or concerns about job security resulting from improvements. Beyond the routine envelope stuffers, poster campaigns, rah-rah sessions, and blurbs in the company newspaper, consider one of the following awareness-elevating approaches:

- Establish a newsletter dedicated to productivity.

- Incorporate productivity reports in advertising and stockholder reports.

- Prepare productivity related "film festivals" for lunch hour and after-work viewing in cafeterias and break areas.

- Incorporate productivity concepts into employee-training programs.

- Provide for productivity factors in job-performance evaluations.

- Sponsor productivity mini-seminars for employees.

Assessing Improvement Opportunities

In Chapter IV we looked at some rather sophisticated techniques you can use to assess improvement opportunities, but what about some less-complicated approaches that can be dealt with by the average manager? Figure 5.8 shows that many factors that affect the organizational climate lead to many improvements. In the opposite sense, deficiencies in some areas may be traced back to climate factors that can, in turn, be changed by adjusting one or more of the controllable factors. Most, if not all,

FIGURE 5.8.

A Productivity Auditing Model.

THINGS MANAGERS CAN DO SOMETHING ABOUT	CURRENT INTERNAL STATE OF THE ORGANIZATION	ORGANIZATIONAL PERFORMANCE
Communication Initiatives	Attitudes	Absenteeism
Employee Involvement	Expectations	Backlogs
Follow Up	Loyalty	Costs
Management Style	Morale	Down-time
Organizational Objectives	Motivational Forces	Efficiency
Organizational Structure	Perceptions	Production
Policies and Procedures	Safety Awareness	Productivity
Staffing Approach	Skill Levels	Product Quality
Technology	Values and Goals	Safety Record
Training	Work Traditions	Turnover

LARGELY PRODUCE   SIGNIFICANTLY INFLUENCE

Source: Huey P. Prater, Company Productivity Manager, Calanese Chemical Co. Adapted from Rensis Likert, *The Human Organization* (New York: McGraw-Hill Book Company, 1967), pp. 26–29.

managers have some influence over the controllable factors. Objectives can be communicated, management styles can be modified, organizations can be restructured, and so on. The main point about these controllable factors is that the adjustment does not have to be done on a corporate level. Begin with the departments or divisions. A lot can be accomplished there.

Technique Selection and Implementation

The implementation of the entire plan, or a portion of it, must be done slowly yet deliberately. Haphazard implementation must be avoided. It is much better to build on small successes than to force wholesale compliance. The greatest threat to successful implementation is "me-too-itis"—the tendency to adopt a technique because your golfing buddy or bridge partner has had success with it. You have to be selective and make sure the technique matches your needs, culture, style, resources, and objectives. Keep in mind the wisdom of some anonymous fisherman who observed,

> It's not the taste of the fisherman that should determine the kind of bait to be used, it's the taste of the fish.

Many managers, and more so consultants, tend to be fishermen. The employees and the organization are the fish.

Rewards and Recognition

Financial reward systems were covered in detail in Chapter III and will not be discussed here. However, we have not presented the case for basic recognition of a job well done. Whether this is accomplished by coffee-mug awards, plaques of appreciation, award banquets, a month's use of a preferred parking place, or displaying one's picture in a prominent location, each recognizes individual achievements. Many large and small companies have had successful recognition programs. The main problem with relying on this approach alone can be summed up by what one employee said, "After twelve coffee mugs and three warm-up jackets, you start looking for something more."

Identifying Improvements

The productivity-measurement systems feed directly into this part of the model. However, other standard measures may be suitable, such as absenteeism, turnover, product quality levels, waste and scrap levels, safety records, backorder levels, and capacity utilization. Any or all of these can be used to identify improvements.

Feedback—To the Employees and to the System

To complete the system, the loop is closed by a feedback step. For individuals it acts to provide recognition. For the system, feedback provides opportunities for modification and fine tuning of the overall approach and techniques used. The continuous flow of feedback data into the organization's steering committee and productivity manager is the foundation for evaluating the system's performance and highlights areas or projects that may need preventative maintenance.

With the loop now closed, the whole process repeats. This was intentional because the productivity-improvement process is continuous and iterative. Problems and difficulties are to be looked upon not as obstacles to progress but rather as opportunities for accomplishment. The feedback provides this opportunity.

Resources for Digging Deeper

Case Studies

Arcata Redwood—Survey Feedback
Atwood Vacuum Machine Co.—Scanlon Plan
Babcock & Wilcox—Quality Circles
Control Data Corporation—Involvement Teams
Corry Jamestown Corporation—Improshare
Honeywell, Incorporated—Suggestion Systems
Shell Oil Company—Team Problem Solving

Sample Position Description of a Productivity Manager
A Directory of Productivity and Quality-of-Work-Life Centers
Companies with Active Productivity or Quality-of-Work-Life
    Programs
A Selected Bibliography

Arcata Redwood Company*
P. O. Box 218
Arcata, California 95521
Telephone: 707/443-5031
Management Contact: Jim Richards
    Director of Personnel, Arcata Forest Products Group

Type of Program: Survey Feedback, Communications
Date Program Initiated: November, 1978
Organizational Unit: Redwood Operation
Number of Employees Involved: Approximately 390
Worker Classification: Nonunion, Exempt and Nonexempt
Structural Characteristics:
    Technology—Manufacturing (Commercial; Some Continuous Process)
    Size—Small
    Degree of Centralization—Centralized
Organizational Climate: Primarily Autocratic

The activities at Arcata Redwood Company illustrate how an employee attitude survey can pinpoint specific organizational needs. In this case, Arcata trained its supervisory personnel in behavior modification to help improve intraorganization communications.

Organizational Background

Arcata Corporation's products and activities consist of printing and printed products; molded containers; and timber and lumber processing. The company produces books, greeting cards, and other paper products; prints magazines, catalogs, directories, brochures, and other commercial work; provides microfilming services for hospitals; and produces molded wood pulp and foam plastic products for the packaging and distribution of food. In 1979, corporate net sales were $579.8 million and net income was nearly $30.5 million.

Arcata owns 76,000 acres of timberland in Northern California, where it conducts timber harvesting, reforestation and milling operations. Arcata Redwood Company, which is part of the Arcata Forest Products Group, is a subsidiary of Arcata Corporation. It was formed in the late 1930s to enter the redwood lumber/logging business. Arcata Redwood has slowly developed into a modern forest products company

---

*© 1980 APC, Inc.

with integrated whitewood/redwood operations. The whitewood operation employs approximately 440 people, while the redwood operations (with which this case study is concerned) employs 390 people.

History and Development of the Program

Arcata Redwood has had a history of low absenteeism, low turnover, nonunion status, good safety records, and positive labor-management relations. However, in late 1978 the vice president of personnel became interested in having an outside consulting firm conduct an attitudinal survey in the company. He suggested this possibility to the president and executive committee. The president of Arcata Redwood wished to learn employees' attitudes toward the company and saw the survey as a means to this knowledge. He issued a memorandum expressing his desire that "*all* operations and staff coordinate and cooperate."

The assessment of employee attitudes through a survey uncovered some deficiencies in the company's employee relations and communications. These results prompted the president to contract further with the same consulting firm for an extensive supervisory/management training program in behavior-modification techniques. Although the company has had long-standing good relations with its employees, its management was seeking yet another tool to strengthen this positive relationship and ensure their nonunion status.

Description of the Program

The survey was administered in November and December of 1978 to all salaried employees and a representative group (one-half) of the hourly employees. It was administered by a consultant from the outside consulting firm to groups of no more than 25 people simultaneously. There were a total of 100 questions, answered on a 5-point scale, which assessed the employees' view of the company in seven major areas. The areas included (1) written policy and communications, (2) performance measurement and feedback, (3) management, (4) problem solving/decision making, (5) self-management, (6) job satisfaction, and (7) job performance.

The survey results were analyzed and compared with national norms for the same survey items. The consultant reported results of the analysis and comparison first to top management, then to all employees of Arcata Redwood. Employees were pleased to see the results and learn how their attitudes compared with those of employees in other organizations. The survey analysis revealed the need for substantial improvements in intraorganization communications, oral instructions, and feedback to employees.

In response to these needs, the president of the company contracted further with the consulting firm for an extensive management-training program in the skills of behavior modification. The program's duration was six months, ending in November of 1979. During these six months, all management personnel (38 individuals) at Arcata Redwood (from the first-line supervisors through the president) met for two hours one night a week with a representative of the consulting firm. The managers were divided into four separate groups (all levels in each group) in order to achieve reasonable-sized groups with which to work. Each group met on a different night. All supervisors were taught the skills of recognizing and positively reinforcing productive behaviors and deemphasizing negative behaviors, such as excess visiting during work hours.

Supervisors were required to practice their skills through on-the-job projects. To pursue the excessive visiting example, a supervisor would not discipline the visiting employee, but choose a method to positively emphasize *not visiting.* The supervisor might call a meeting of all those employees who work well and use their time productively just to thank them for the good job they do. Another method of approaching the problem is to measure the group's output and simply report it to them. In these instances, the group members are usually surprised at their low output rate. Therefore, they increase their performance immediately, reducing the amount of time spent visiting. This increased performance is typically a lasting change, rather than a transient one. If the latter strategy is chosen and behavior favorably changes, the supervisor then positively reinforces the involved subordinate(s).

During the six-month training, there were two additional workshops—one approximately midway through the training program and one near the end. Each workshop lasted two and a half days. These workshops afforded the managers the opportunity to practice their new management skills with the observation and feedback of the outside consultants. During this time, everyone had opportunities to role play with everyone else (from the first-line supervisors through the president).

Since completion of the training, many supervisors have continued using behavior-modification techniques with their subordinates. Emphasis is on positively communicating with their employees. Supervisors who continue to use the techniques have various feedback projects in operation. Maintenance of the program entails a one-day workshop each year with the managers and outside consultants. Costs of the program were approximately $110,000, including administration and assessment of the survey and six months of consultant time for the training program. The one-day maintenance workshops will add further costs.

Problems

Difficulties encountered have stemmed from resistance to change on the part of upper and middle management. From the exploration stage through the entire program one particular member of the upper-management team was in opposition to all activities. His position was that his management style had been effective thus far and he saw no reason to change. He did participate in the survey and training activities in response to the president's stance on the program.

Since the training program, first-line managers have been the primary group to continue utilizing the behavior-modification techniques, communicating with their subordinates. Middle and upper management, for the most part, have reverted to the management styles they utilized prior to the training. It is unclear at this point how this problem will be handled, if at all.

Results

Impacts of the program fall into three areas: financial, productivity, and employee morale. Results have not been measured on a company-wide basis; however, some isolated changes have been measured.

Financially, management feels the program has been more than justified through cost savings. One example is the reduced cost of workers' compensation to the company. Since supervisors have been working more closely with their employees, workers have become more safety conscious. This has resulted in reduced accidents to such an extent that from 1978 to 1979 Arcata Redwood's cost of workers' compensation dropped 8%, while, according to the Consumer Price Index, the costs of medical care rose 14.6%. Management has also noticed that employees are more concerned with energy conservation, as they turn off machines and lights when appropriate.

Improvements have likewise been seen in productivity and quality. One chop line (which is a production line) increased its output by 40%, while changing from a nine-hour to an eight-hour shift. In another case, at one of the logging sites a crew increased its yard production by 20%. In terms of quality, one grade-standards crew decreased its percentage of misgraded boards from 10% to 4%. Each of these three improvements occurred in only one day as a result of precise feedback from supervisors. The improvements were not short lived, but have been maintained at the increased level.

Upper management has also noticed an improved employee morale. Since the attitudinal survey, many more employees go to the personnel office simply to ask questions or communicate concerns. Employees seem to feel much more comfortable communicating to management. In addition, even though the company is nonunionized, it has had a grievance procedure for its employees since early 1976. There have been no grievances since the management training program ended. Prior to that time two or three grievances a month were commonplace.

Future Plans

Although there are no extensive plans for the future, the top-management group is currently examining the possibility of establishing a number of committees. The committee structure, if established, would provide a vehicle for directing employees' efforts to solve work-related problems.

Atwood Vacuum Machine Co.*
1400 Eddy Avenue
Rockford, IL 61101
Telephone: 815/877-5771
Management Contact: James H. Rilott, Vice President,
    Corporate Industrial Relations

Type of Plan: Scanlon plan
Date Plan Installed: 1954
Size of Unit Covered by Plan: Entire company (7 plants)
Number of Employees: 1900
Type of Operation: Manufacturing
Type of Worker: Union and nonunion
Structural Characteristics: Mass/unit technology, large, centralized
Organizational Climate: Consultative

The case study at Atwood reflects the structure of a typical Scanlon plan. There are several notable characteristics. The plan: (1) has been used for 25 years, (2) has been consistently correlated with increasing productivity and consequently good bonuses, (3) reflects the success of one company in using a company-wide plan to solve its problem with an individual-incentives plan, and (4) represents a case in which both union and nonunion employees are covered under the same labor ratio. Management credits the Scanlon plan with creating a climate in which jobs may be transferred to different plants without union complaints.

Company History

Atwood Vacuum Machine Company is a privately owned company with total sales of approximately $100 million. The company is divided into two divisions. The Automotive Division controls five plants and manufactures original equipment for cars, internal body hardware, and custom stampings. These products have generally been preordered through contracts with automotive manufacturers. The second division, Mobile Products Division, has two plants and produces appliances for recreational vehicles and hardware and brake systems for recreational vehicles, mobile homes, and agricultural machines. Following production, the products are marketed by the division.

---

*©1980 APC, Inc.

Management and Production Climate

The worker-management relationship is characterized by a participative management style and good worker attitudes. Historically, there have been very few worker grievances, and no cases of work stoppage. The production climate is characterized by a moderate degree of technology with the emphasis on product quality varying somewhat across product lines.

Prior Incentives Program

Prior to the Scanlon plan, the company had used an individual incentives program based on piecework. This program included less than one-half of the workers. For those included, there was controversy over the piecerates and limited production due to the fear of rate changes. For those workers not included, there was little incentive. Generally this led to a climate of conflict between the piecerate workers and the supportive personnel. Moreover, it was noted that the time studies necessary for installing the piecerate system were quite expensive.

Development of the Plan

Atwood Vacuum Company began to look for a different incentive plan primarily because of the problems it experienced with the piecerate system. This problem identification and the subsequent discussion of alternative plans were conducted by the top management. At that time, the company's president believed strongly in the potential of his workers to contribute to the company. Whether as a direct or indirect consequence, the decision was made to implement a Scanlon plan. Throughout the planning phases, the union was kept informed but did not participate directly.

Implementation of the Plan

This plan was implemented through a series of explanatory meetings with management, workers, and union. Following these meetings a general election was held to install the plan for a trial year (1954). The percentage of workers in favor was 78%. This increased to 98% when the vote was taken the following year to implement the plan on a permanent basis. The initial resistance to the plan apparently stemmed from the belief that the labor ratio would be manipulative. This later gave way to a great deal of trust.

Plan Description

The plan operates much like the typical Scanlon plan. All employees in both the plants and the office participate. There are the usual production and screening committees with their management and worker representatives. Production-committee worker representatives are elected by each department, while plant-wide elections are held for screening-committee members. Each committee meets once a month and performs the usual functions. The responsibilities of each committee member are specified in a written document which describes the plan. In regard to these functions, the production-committee's chairman, the department supervisor, is allowed to spend up to $200 in implementing suggestions. All suggestions are written and are published monthly.

Incentive Bonus

The bonus system also reflects the typical Scanlon plan. The labor ratio is based on historical data and includes (1) the direct labor content, (2) the indirect labor content, (3) the salary payroll, and (4) the volume of production. "Bonuses are paid monthly based on improvements in productivity (beating the labor ratio)." From each month's bonus, 25% is held in reserve for possible deficit months. From the remaining 75%, the employees receive 75% immediately, and the company receives 25%. The monthly bonuses are announced at the screening committee meetings and are then posted. At the end of the Scanlon fiscal year (which in this case is tied to the car-model year), the reserve is distributed on the same 75%–25% basis. At the same time, an annual review of the labor ratio is conducted by the accounting department. The review evaluates the extent and the impact of changes in the following areas: (1) wages, (2) forecasted volume, (3) product mix, (4) prices, (5) direct labor, indirect labor, and salary payroll, and (6) technology. The accounting department's review is later evaluated by management and a consultant.

Results

Since the installation of the plan, bonus payments have averaged 12.5%. More recently from 1971–1980, the average was 14.8% and for 1978, it was 21.25%. In 1980 the average bonus payment was 5%. This significant drop is attributable to the decline in automobile sales and Atwood's association through the automobile division. The number of suggestions have averaged 2500/year and have ranged between 2000 and 3000. Generally, 70–75% of these suggestions have been implemented. Since the plan's installation, the base ratio has been relatively stable while showing a steady decline from 30% to approximately 26%. During poor business cycles, it was noted that bonuses were harder to make, but even so, management felt that it was during these times that the plan was particularly valuable. In general, the company feels that the Scanlon plan has directly and positively contributed to their "growth, competitiveness, product quality, and employee relations." Minor problems concerned the difficulty which some managers had in adopting the philosophy of the plan. More importantly, it was noted that when changes had to be made in the bonus ratio, such changes demanded careful explanation.

Evaluation

Overall, both workers and management strongly support the plan. The important factors creating this support include the bonuses as well as the feelings by workers and lower-level managers that they are confided in and given more responsibility. In this, its 26th year of existence, the Scanlon plan at Atwood is still maintained by a combination of "(1) management commitment and belief, (2) employee education, (3) recognition, and (4) communications and publicity."

Babcock & Wilcox*

Quality & Technology Division
P. O. Box 351
Barberton, Ohio 44203
Telephone: 216/753-4511
Management Contacts: Robert P. Meyer, Participative Task Teams
    Coordinator

Type of Program: Participative Task Teams (Quality Circles)
Date Program Initiated: September 1, 1978
Company Units: Nuclear Equipment Division and Tubular Products
    Division
Number of Employees Involved: 9 teams of 5–10 employees
    each
Worker Classification: Salaried and Hourly
Structural Characteristics:
    Technology—Manufacturing
    Size—Large
    Degree of Centralization—Decentralized

    Through the Participative Task Teams program at Babcock & Wilcox, employees meet in groups to identify, analyze, and solve work-related problems. The company has realized both tangible and intangible results.

Organizational Background

The Babcock & Wilcox Company is a wholly owned subsidiary of the J. Ray McDermott Company, Inc. B&W is a major international supplier of energy systems, engineered materials, and industrial automation systems for utility, industrial, commercial, marine, and government applications. Annual sales exceed $2 billion and there are approximately 40,000 employees located in 24 nations.

    Management style is progressive. Attitude surveys, performance appraisals, and job analyses are regularly conducted. Employees of the divisions with which this case study is concerned are represented by the International Brotherhood of Boilermakers, Iron Shipbuilders, Blacksmiths, Forgers and Helpers and the United Steel Workers.

---

*©1980 APC, Inc.

History and Development of the Program

In 1977, the General Manager of the Nuclear Equipment Division expressed a desire at the corporate level to institute a group problem-solving program within his division. The Director of Quality was likewise interested in this area of organization improvement and responded. B&W hired an additional quality engineer, who has also become the Participative Task Teams (PTT) coordinator. These latter two individuals researched employee involvement in the area and visited domestic, as well as foreign, organizations with quality circle programs.

Babcock and Wilcox bought quality circle training materials from outside consultants. The director of quality and the task teams coordinator then adapted the materials to fit the needs of the nuclear equipment division.

A PTT steering committee, consisting of department managers, a union representative, and the program facilitator, was formed. This committee determined the scope of the pilot program, how task-team leaders and members would be chosen, team size, whether there would be only blue-collar teams, and finally, meeting times and locations. Meeting weekly, the steering committee had extensive involvement in the program during the first two or three months.

Description of the Program

Participative Task Teams (PTT) is a management-supported, employee group motivation/problem-solving program which was pilot tested in the nuclear equipment division of the power generation group of Babcock & Wilcox Company. The program has been expanded to the entire division which has about 1500 employees, as well as the tubular products division. The program is a form of participative management or job enrichment in which employees meet in groups to identify, analyze, and solve work-related problems.

Coordination is provided by the central quality assurance department. Divisional coordination comes from the PTT steering committee and the personnel department. The union representative serves on the steering committee in an advisory role. The steering committee, which initially met weekly, now meets once a month to review the effectiveness of the program and plan its future expansion. A facilitator plans the meetings and handles room arrangements and supplies.

First-line supervisors serve as team leaders. They attend 24 hours of training conducted by the PTT coordinator. The leaders, in turn, conduct eight one-hour training sessions for team members. Team participation is voluntary, but supervisors encourage their employees to join so they may become involved in decision making.

Teams of 5–10 workers meet with their supervisor one hour per week on company time. They attempt to solve problems in their immediate work areas, using the quality circle techniques such as Pareto analysis, brainstorming, cause-and-effect diagrams, and management presentations. Team members are also interested in economic calculations, so that cost reductions can be identified.

Originally, the division had two teams of salaried employees and four teams of hourly employees. Since September, 1978, those numbers have grown to include four salaried teams and eight hourly teams.

Recognition is given to team members by management involvement in team presentations, company newspapers, and sharing in monetary rewards via the employee suggestion program.

Problems

Team leaders have indicated that they have had trouble finding extra time for the program. The concept of coleaders is being encouraged to relieve this pressure. A second problem has been that some middle managers do not want to release their problems to employee teams. They believe their own staffs should handle the problems.

Results

Preliminary costs were the result of up-front planning, purchase of training materials, and team members' time at meetings. They are estimated to have been less than $50,000 for the first six months.

The director of quality reports that benefits to B&W have been both tangible and intangible. The company has seen no loss in productivity as a result of the team meetings. In addition, an employee-attitude survey was administered seven months after the pilot program began. Survey results indicated improved morale and improved personal productivity.

Control Data Corporation*
8100—34th Avenue South
Box 0
Minneapolis, MN 55440
Phone: 612/853-5429
Management Contacts: Don Gilbertsen—Manager, Involvement Teams
    Dave Dille—Manager, Plans and Controls

Type of Program: Involvement Teams (Quality Circles)
Date Plan Initiated: December, 1977
Company Units: 40 teams in portions of 11 different plants (as of
    6-1-80)
Number of Employees Involved: Approximately 360
Worker Classification: Salaried and hourly workers
Structural Characteristics:
    Technology—Manufacturing
    Size—Large
    Degree of Centralization—Decentralized

Involvement teams at Control Data have been very successful, growing from one pilot team at the end of 1977 to 40 teams in mid-1980. The program offers employees the opportunity to deal with work-related problems and concerns through brainstorming and problem solving.

Company Background

Control Data Corporation is a publicly owned corporation occupied in the application of its computing technology, financial resources, and consulting services. The organization has two main activities—the computer business and financial services. There are roughly 58,000 employees in 47 countries. In 1979 the corporate earnings were $124 million. Roughly two-thirds of this figure was generated by the computer business, the arm of Control Data with which this case is concerned.

Control Data is essentially a nonunionized organization. None of the areas now employing the involvement team program are unionized. Overall management style has been aggressive, providing an authoritative, rather than participative, atmosphere.

*©1980 APC, Inc.

History and Development of the Program

Top-level management interest in production programs, cost reduction, and team development resulted in the initial 1977 discussions of a possible quality-circles program. There was a desire to more efficiently utilize human resources within the company.

Management decided to proceed with the establishment of a pilot team in December of 1977. Another pilot team was begun in July, 1978, at a second plant. Both teams were involved in manufacturing. In the establishment of these two teams, employees were given a general introduction to the concept of quality circles, after which some employees volunteered to participate as team members. Two managers were selected and trained to serve as team leaders for these initial groups. All training was, and is still, conducted by internal trainers. These two pilot teams were successful. Thus, in November, 1978, management decided to support the creation of more teams and the development of more extensive leader and management training.

Program Description

An involvement team is a small group of employees (average of 10 members) who do similar work. The team members voluntarily meet weekly, on company time, to review problems and concerns related to their work in an attempt to discover solutions to the problems. Areas considered in these meetings include productivity, quality, communications, etc. Areas which are not addressed by teams are those of salaries and benefits, hiring/firing policies, and personalities. The team recommends their solutions to management, implementing solutions themselves if possible.

Each team has a leader who is a manager trained for the role of team leader through a two-day session. The team leaders are trained by the team administrators in involvement techniques. Team leaders in turn train the team members in goal setting, brainstorming, etc. These people are responsible for the operation of their teams.

There are currently two involvement team administrators working with the program—one full-time, one part-time. These two people have a wide range of responsibilities. They develop necessary training materials and conduct training and orientation sessions for team leaders. They also work closely with the steering committee, maintain records, and serve as the interface between the teams and other company organizations.

The largest division of Control Data, which has approximately half of the teams, also has a steering committee composed of the division management personnel. The committee's function involves administrative decisions and general direction of the program. It is concerned with such issues as how many teams should be established, where they should be established, etc.

Management support is demonstrated through provision of time, space, and materials necessary for team meetings. Support also takes the form of encouraging employees to attend scheduled team activities. The management responds to team requests and solutions expediently, implementing approved solutions and providing detailed explanations for denial of requests. A manager may also suggest problems for team consideration.

Direct costs of the involvement-team program have not been documented. However, the involvement team manager works full-time as involvement team administrator. There is also a half-time administrator in the largest division. In addition, there is the expense of the training notebooks and other training materials. But these costs are considered minimal by the company when the benefits of the program are noted.

No differences in production are noticed as a result of the work time lost in the weekly team meetings. Therefore there is no apparent cost to the company here.

Results

There has been no formal evaluation of the program, but rather it is judged on the basis of the general well being of the organization. There has been no attempt to gather statistical results because it is considered very difficult to discriminate what portion of improvements is attributable to involvement teams as opposed to other aspects of the company "people development" orientation.

Every six months a review meeting is held between management and employees involved in the program. At this meeting highlights and progress of the past months are reviewed.

Benefits reported by Control Data's management include improved management-worker relations, improved communication, increased productivity, higher quality work, and improved employee performance. The employees are enjoying the opportunity of self-expression, problem solving, and seeing action taken as a result of their suggestions. Employees are enthusiastic and take pride in being recognized. They feel they have considerable control over the quality and efficiencies of the work they are doing.

Future Plans

Control Data has no definition of how far the involvement-teams program may reach. There is a long-range focus on developing teams and learning from experiences. Two or three teams are being added each month in a variety of areas including professional, clerical, payroll, test areas, etc. There is an aim to gain broad experiences and perspectives from these varied groups. Future plans also include development of involvement teams in some of the unionized areas of the corporation.

Corry Jamestown Corporation, Division Hon Industries*

Corry, PA 16407
Telephone: 814/664-4611
Management Contact: Bill Sample, Manufacturing Manager

Type of Plan: Improshare
Date Plan Installed: February, 1978
Company Unit Covered by Plan: All hourly personnel
Number of Employees Covered: Approximately 570
Type of Worker: Union
Structural Characteristics: Medium-sized; batch processing
Organizational Climate: Very participative

Company Background

Corry Jamestown is a wholly owned subsidiary of Hon Industries, a manufacturer of office furniture. In 1978, Hon Industries' net sales were almost $184 million. Net income was nearly $15 million. Hon is the second largest office furniture manufacturer in the United States.

Located in Corry, Pennsylvania, Corry Jamestown produces high-quality metal office furniture including desks, chairs, files, and systems. The company employs in excess of 570 people. Production and maintenance workers are represented by Local #1097, District #65 of the International Association of Machinists and Aerospace Workers.

The company primarily consists of batch processing of sheet metal including cutting, welding, etc. The seating division works with other materials as well, including fabrics, vinyl, and wood. The seating division is one of only two divisions. The other is the furniture division. Management style at Corry Jamestown is consultative.

History and Development of the Program

Union-management relations at Corry Jamestown have had a fluctuating history. After numerous years of poor relations with a number of unresolved grievances, the 1975 negotiations terminated in a major 9-week strike. Representatives of the Federal Conciliation and Mediation Service helped settle the strike. Afterwards, union and company representatives met separately and jointly with the Jamestown area labor/management coordinator to explore the avenues which would benefit both parties. Following a series of meetings, the labor/management committee at Corry Jamestown was formed. Presently, this committee is composed of the union-negotiating committee and four man-

---

*©1981 APC, Inc.

agement members—the president, the executive vice president, the factory manager, and the director of industrial relations.

Initial successful areas of action for this committee included clarifying a holiday qualifier clause in the contract and creating a new job evaluation procedure and an employee-of-the-month program. There were unsuccessful efforts in improving the seniority and suggestion systems. The resolution of the latter problem came later with implementation of Improshare. Each of these areas was dealt with by an individual subcommittee during the remainder of 1975, through 1976, and into 1977.

However, management interest seemed to ebb in 1977 and monthly meetings were cancelled. This led to union withdrawal from the labor/management committee in the fall of 1977. Thus, the two parties again came together and discussed the issues of concern and commitment to labor-management cooperation. After several meetings management again stated its commitment to the cooperative efforts.

As a result of Corry Jamestown's history of low productivity, management was interested in improving productivity through an employee-incentive program. A top-management team explored a variety of such programs including Scanlon, Rucker, Work Factors, and Improshare. This team concluded that the Improshare plan best fit the company's situation.

Corry Jamestown invited a consultant to Corry to make Improshare presentations separately to union and management leaders. An Improshare plan was created for the company and the labor/management committee decided to sponsor it. Management presented the program to all hourly employees. Officers of the union-negotiating committee were present for each presentation. Each presentation took approximately an hour with a video tape describing the plan shown during the first half hour. The second half of each session was devoted to answering labor's questions. A great number of questions were directed toward union officials who were in support of the program. The 50/50 profit split between labor and management particularly appealed to employees. The plan was implemented in February of 1978.

Program Description

The labor-management organization of Corry Jamestown is headed by the labor/management committee which oversees all joint activities. It is not only responsible for all Improshare activities, but also supervises project task forces which are not formally part of the Improshare plan. These task forces work on special and specific projects including Improshare.

A permanent Improshare administrative committee exists to assure that the plan functions according to the Improshare plan guidelines. There are a total of 6 members on this committee—3 labor representatives and 3 management representatives.

There is also a plant-productivity subcommittee concerned with productivity problems and projects in the plant. This committee has 8 members including the plant manager, the plant superintendent, the chief manufacturing engineer, and labor representatives from various manufacturing functional groups. This committee reviews suggestions and solutions developed by departmental teams. Both the Improshare administrative committee and the plant productivity subcommittee meet weekly.

Corry Jamestown has 9 departmental teams who either meet formally or informally, as they choose, weekly. They identify problems and concerns in their department, deal directly with the problems when possible, and refer other problems with team suggestions for resolution to the plant productivity subcommittee. The teams are usually composed of a supervisor and 2 or 3 elected labor representatives.

Results

Overall productivity improvement in 1978 was 17.2%, resulting in an 8.6% Improshare payout to employees. The productivity improvement for 1979 was 17.4% with an 8.7% Improshare payout.

The formulas for both productivity improvement and payout are standard Improshare calculations.

The plan has been very well received by the employees. They contribute to productivity improvements and are interested in the overall results of the plan. A weekly publication keeps them informed. The Improshare plan at Corry Jamestown has helped create a positive atmosphere as well as improve productivity.

Honeywell, Incorporated*

Address: Honeywell Plaza
Minneapolis, Minnesota 55408
Telephone: 612/870-2836
Management Contact: Leo Kirk, S.T.E.P. Program Manager

Type of Program: Suggestion program
Date Program Initiated: 1942, with major changes in 1965
Company Units: Corporate offices and four divisions in Minneapolis
Number of Employees Involved: 10,222
Worker Classification: Hourly, Nonexempt
Structural Characteristics:
>   Technology—Manufacturing (mass production)
>   Size—Medium
>   Degree of Centralization—Decentralized
Organizational Climate: Consultative

The program at Honeywell is a well-established and successful suggestion program. Its success is attributable primarily to management's continued active support.

Organizational Background

Honeywell, Incorporated, is a publicly owned company engaged in the design, manufacture, sale, and service of automation equipment and systems which utilize many types of information to produce some type of output, control, or display. Its major divisions are environmental systems and controls, industrial systems and controls, aerospace and defense, and information systems. In 1979 Honeywell had sales of over $4.2 billion, and a net income of $261 million.

History and Development of the Program

Honeywell's suggestion plan was started in 1942. It operated on a par with other systems at that time, but because of the changing times and new programs with different motivational approaches, several changes were made. At that time, 3 major revisions were made in the plan.

---

*©1980 APC, Inc.

Prior to 1965, suggestion forms were deposited anonymously in a standard suggestion box where they were picked up by a suggestion administrator or sent through company mail to the suggestion office. The identity of the suggestor was removed and the suggestion sent to the proper investigator. In 1965 Honeywell replaced the anonymous form with one that had to be signed and given directly to the suggester's supervisor. This change has significantly improved communication between employees and supervisors. A second and more significant change was tying the performance evaluation of supervisors to the suggestion plan. Supervisors were given goals for the number of employee suggestions they should receive, process, and implement. Part of their performance evaluation was their success in achieving these goals. This technique has motivated supervisors to get involved and has been a significant factor in the success of Honeywell's plan. The third improvement was increased communication with the employee while his suggestion is being processed. He was contacted personally when he submitted his suggestion, during its evaluation, and at the time of its acceptance or rejection. This tactic has been very helpful in the success of Honeywell's suggestion program. (The personal-contact approach at several stages in the suggestion-system process is not widely used by American industry. Many companies contact the employee by letter during the process.)

Description of the Program

The suggestion plan covers all hourly and nonexempt employees in Minneapolis, including the corporate offices and the avionics, defense system, commercial, and residential divisions. To be eligible for consideration, all suggestions must be outside the employee's area of responsibility.

Honeywell has 20 to 25 office and factory subcommittees, composed of 2 or 3 people, which approve suggestions with awards of under $100. If the award is $100 or more the suggestion goes to the board of judges for approval. This board has seven members from the various divisions and specialties within the company. Awards of $5 to $100 are presented to the employee by his supervisor. When larger awards are made, 2 levels of supervision must be present.

First-line supervisors are heavily involved in the plan. They are responsible for assisting employees in writing suggestions. In addition, they either investigate and evaluate the suggestions themselves or refer them to a more qualified person. In 1979 the average suggestion required two hours of investigation.

From 1965 to 1977 Honeywell's maximum award for a suggestion was $1000. In 1977 it was raised to $1500, and subsequently to

$2500 on February 1, 1979. This is a relatively small maximum award, but it is consistent with Honeywell's philosophy that a large award is not nearly as important as the recognition employees receive from a successful suggestion. Management believes that there is no correlation between the amount of the maximum award and the number of suggestions submitted by employees.

Honeywell does, however, have some small incentives that complement the monetary awards. In 1979 every employee received a gold pen in recognition of his first suggestion of the year. When Honeywell realized $150 savings from one or more suggestions, the employee was given a security light for his home. When the company savings reached $500 the employee was given a $20 gift certificate. Honeywell believes that these small incentives stimulate and sustain interest in the program and has continued similar programs through 1979.

Results

The National Association of Suggestion Systems ranks Honeywell's program as one of the most successful in the country. It has been presented national awards for the excellence of its system for seven years in a row. In 1979, Honeywell received 221 suggestions per 100 eligible employees, which is far above the N.A.S.S. average of 15 suggestions per 100 employees. In the same year, Honeywell had an employee participation rate of 46%, more than double the N.A.S.S. average of 20%. Finally, Honeywell awarded 49% of its suggestions in 1979, compared to the average of 24% reported by N.A.S.S.

Currently, Honeywell has 6 to 8 different suggestion programs in effect throughout the corporation. The corporate officers encourage them but leave it to the individual divisions to develop their own programs. A few divisions in Honeywell offer a $25,000 maximum award.

Honeywell attributes the success of its programs to 3 factors: (1) the strong, demonstrated support of management throughout the year, (2) the involvement of first-line supervisors, and (3) employee recognition.

Additional Programs

Honeywell in Minneapolis also has a program called Strive Towards Error-Free Performance (STEP). It is run in conjunction with the suggestion plan but stresses error reduction on the job.

Honeywell also has over 300 successfully operating team circles (quality circles) throughout the corporation. The company has found that the two programs are complementary and mutually supportive.

Company: Honeywell

Suggestion Plan Fact Sheet — 1979

Program Started	1942
# of Employees	13,949
# of Eligible Employees	10,222
# of Suggestions Received	22,619
# Received/100 Employees	221
# Employees Submitting	4,748
# Employees Submitting/ 100 Employees	46
# Suggestions Awarded	10,484
% Suggestions Awarded	49%
Total Award Payments	$320,609
Average Award Given	$30.58
Highest Award Given	$2,500 (max)
Total Tangible Savings	$1,729,954
$ Savings/Award	$165.01
$ Savings/100 Employees	16,924
Cost of Program	589,901
Savings to Cost Ratio	2.9:1
Average Processing Time	75 days
Award Based on	1st year savings
Award Payment basis	17% of gross
Minimum Award	$5.00
Maximum Award	$2500.00
Intangible Award System	Yes
Eligibility	All hourly, nonexempt, up to $1600/mo.
Department System Attached to	Industrial eng.
Plan Administrator Reports to	Industrial eng.
Who Evaluates Suggestions	Line mgmt.
Contact with Suggestor:	
At Acknowledgment	Personal
During Evaluation	Personal
At Nonadoption	Personal
Award Presented by	Supervision and mgmt.

Shell Oil Company*
One Shell Plaza
Houston, Texas 77001
Phone: 713/241-5834
Management Contact: Frank Douma, Employee Relations Associate

Type of Program: Team Problem Solving (SPIRIT)
Date Program Initiated: 1975
Organizational Units: Information Center, Head Office in Houston, Credit Card Center in Tulsa, and Administrative Centers in U. S. Cities
Number of Employees Involved: 1800
Worker Classification: Clerical, office support, and data processing
Structural Characteristics:
  Technology—Professional/Service
  Size—Small, Medium, and Large
  Degree of Centralization—Varies by Function
Organizational Climate: Too varied to classify

Shell's implementation of SPIRIT, a team approach to problem solving, was initiated in 1975 to effect a change in low morale experienced by employees at its information center in Houston. Shell management indicates that SPIRIT has improved the morale of its participants and stimulated interest among other Shell offices in using the program.

Organizational Background

Shell Oil and its subsidiaries are engaged in the acquisition and development of oil and gas lands; in the production, purchase, sale, transportation, and refining of crude oil; and in the transportation and marketing of its products, principally gasoline, lubricating oils, distillates, and residuals. The company also manufactures and sells chemical products and produces, transports, treats, and sells natural gas. In 1979 Shell had a gross income of $14.5 billion and a net income of $1.1 billion.

The Shell information center houses the company's principal computing and data-processing function. Approximately 2,000 people are employed in planning, programming, scheduling, accounting, transportation, and supply. Shell's credit card center in Tulsa and administrative centers located in 7 U. S. cities employ approximately 3,000 people. All Shell companies including Shell Oil Company, Shell Chemical, Shell Pipeline, and Shell Development are serviced out of the Houston information center.

History and Development of the Program

Shell's SPIRIT Program is a problem-solving technique employing a team approach. The name is an acronym for Shell's Program for Improvement Recognizing Individual's Talents.

SPIRIT was started in 1975 when the manager of administrative services at the information center was seeking a solution to the problem of low morale among some of his 200–300 employees. The low morale was evidenced by an excessive turnover rate and strong negativeness that became apparent through individual conversations.

The basic material for SPIRIT was developed by Shell but is based on industrial engineering work-simplification procedures. Shell's exposure to this came from seminars held by an outside consultant.

Description of the Program

Employees selected as trainers initially attend six three-hour sessions. At these video-taped sessions employees learn the five fundamental steps to solving problems on the job. These steps are:

1. Select a job
2. Get the facts
3. Challenge every detail
4. Develop improved method
5. Install improved method

The trainers then provide five two-hour sessions for employees who want to participate in the plan. It must be emphasized that all training and team membership is voluntary. Employees are not required to join a team after they receive problem-solving training. They may make individual suggestions on a problem without being part of a team.

Teams are encouraged to meet regularly, usually weekly or bi-weekly. Their problem-solving and work-simplification activities need not be limited to their own department. Team activities are encouraged by the supervisor or manager of the area, but supervisory staff must not dominate the team. Solutions are studied and arrived at democratically.

Team leadership is rotated in one of three ways: chronologically, by problem area, or by vote of the members. Ordinarily, groups or individuals who have submitted suggestions receive feedback from management within 10 working days.

Employees receive no financial awards for accepted suggestions. Recognition is provided through publicity in local and corporatewide publications. Significant individual and team accomplishments are recognized by plaque awards.

Cost savings realized from suggestions are not stressed. The suggestion form is simple and teams are required to document their activities only minimally.

The initial out-of-pocket costs of implementing SPIRIT in 1975 was estimated to be $4000, including all visual aids and written material. True costs, including salaries, were not collected because in-house printing, video taping and script writing were not included as program costs. A comparable program today, purchasing all outside services, would cost at least $10,000.

Problems

Some team problem-solving failures had occurred earlier at Shell in a work simplification program called "job improvement" (1969–71). There appeared to be two major causes for failures. First, group leadership was too disciplined, causing a decline in interest and participation levels. Second, at the beginning of the program, upper management issued instructions to individuals and passed by middle management. Shell now feels that middle and first-line supervisors must be included in the program. They are believed to be an essential link in the training and leadership of teams and in the overall growth of team activities. SPIRIT attempted to address these problem areas.

SPIRIT got off to a slow start due to an overestimation of the ability of the supervisors to perform the training function. This deficiency was corrected with the development of extensive audio-visual materials to assist supervisors in their training of team members. This method now requires reduced preparation and teaching on the part of the supervisors.

Results

Since its inception, the program has grown to include some 1800 employees in the information center, the head office in Houston, the credit card center in Tulsa, as well as administrative centers in 7 U. S. cities. The following table gives an idea of the program results from 1975–1977:

Year	Personnel Trained	Number of of Teams	Suggestions Presented	Percent Implemented
1975	247	33	240	80%
1976	472	42	387	77%
1977	1,036	48	571	76%

Although all statistics are not available, growth in 1978 slowed significantly and only 150 additional personnel were trained with no significant change in the number of teams over 1977. This may be due to a saturation effect and the voluntary nature of team participation. The fact that training in the SPIRIT techniques is voluntary may have contributed to the decline. However, early 1979 and 1980 activity indicates a reversal of this trend, and the training of a significantly larger number of personnel is anticipated but not to the level experienced in 1977.

These offices have not been required by upper management to report the various statistics after 1977. Management wishes employees to have complete control and authority over the organization and function of their program. It is believed that a requirement to submit statistics was viewed as "outside" pressure from management, thus reducing employee "ownership" of the program.

National and local attention to the need for productivity improvement (through APC and others) has stimulated requests by other Shell offices for SPIRIT. Although there has been no formal measurement or tracking of the change in morale at Shell's information center, management indicates that morale of SPIRIT participants has improved significantly.

SAMPLE Position Description

Position: Corporate Director, Productivity Improvement
Reports To: Vice President, Management Information Systems

General Function

The purpose of this position is to lead the productivity-improvement and develop, implement, and maintain it by providing direction, guidelines, coordination, communications, and training services. The objective is to assure that all managers are knowledgeable and supportive of the program and that intelligent efforts are made to meet company productivity goals.

Specific Duties

1. Direct the activities of the Productivity Improvement Program (PIP) so that it serves as an effective means of improving productivity throughout the corporation.

2. Develop and/or cause to be developed specific productivity measures for individual functions, divisions, and the corporation to provide basis for monitoring results at all levels.

3. Prepare and publish state-of-the-art productivity-improvement information for use by all company managers.

4. Conduct productivity meetings, seminars, and workshops throughout the company.

5. Establish and maintain a company "library" on productivity ideas, facts, goals, visual aids, etc.

6. Coordinate with company-wide employee motivation programs so that they enhance the company Productivity Improvement Program (PIP).

7. Establish methods to monitor low productivity factors and develop and recommend corrective actions.

8. Assist the productivity steering committee in evaluating the effectiveness of the productivity-improvement program.

9. Prepare quarterly reports illustrating results of PIP's throughout the company.

SAMPLE Position Description

Position: Company Productivity Manager
Reports To: President

1. Provide leadership and direction to all functions relative to the selection and installation of productivity-improvement techniques, and manage these efforts in order to achieve desired goals and objectives.

2. Actively pursue engineering, manufacturing, and construction to coordinate the production of product designs that facilitate manufacturing and construction within cost and margin objectives.

3. Serve as chairperson of the productivity coordination committee responsible for the establishment and/or implementation of: productivity objectives, productivity-measurement guidelines, projects to increase employee involvement and improved quality of work life, a forum for sharing productivity improvement problems and concerns.

4. Establish a method for measuring and reporting on productivity gains and performance.

5. Coordinate with all functional units to establish and implement policies and procedures which improve the quality of work life of all employees while increasing functional productivity.

6. Provide for improved employee awareness of the general productivity situation and its importance and impact on the economy, inflation, and other areas of interest.

7. Maintain and update skills and expertise relative to the state of the art in productivity programs and techniques.

8. Perform assigned duties and responsibilities within the established expense budgets.

9. Provide input to corporate business plans and goals.

10. Other duties and responsibilities as may be assigned.

SAMPLE Position Description

Position: Productivity Coordinator
Reports To: President

OBJECTIVE

To establish a central focus for encouraging and monitoring the productivity-improvement program of the organization.

RESPONSIBILITIES

1. Chairs and coordinates all activities of the productivity team leaders' committee.

2. Reports to the president in this function.

3. Acts as facilitator for all teams.

4. Arranges and attends all presentations to management.

5. Assigns new staff members to productivity teams.

6. Arranges training directed toward improved productivity.

7. Prepares quarterly status reports.

8. Measures productivity using statistics, ratios, and other tools approved by management.

9. Expends approximately 10 hours per week on this position.

10. Maintains awareness and monitors staff and quality of work life.

11. Holds the assignment for 6 months as it is an employee development position.

12. Manages the productivity-improvement budget.

SAMPLE Position Description

Position: Productivity Coordinator

Reports To: Director, Human Resources

Major Responsibility: Coordinate all productivity-improvement efforts within the company and serve as an internal consultant on productivity.

Other Responsibilities:

(1) Improve awareness of productivity within the company.

(2) Assist all units in establishing productivity-improvement programs.

(3) Conduct productivity appraisals in all units.

(4) Assure that sound productivity measures and goals are established within the company.

(5) Establish a system for monitoring and reporting company productivity.

(6) Develop and maintain expertise on all the latest productivity-improvement programs and techniques.

(7) Maintain liaison with external organizations in all matters relative to the organization.

A Directory of Productivity and Quality-of-Work-Life Centers

American Center for Quality of Work Life
3301 New Mexico Avenue N.W.
Suite 202
Washington DC 22016
(202) 338-2933

American Institute of Industrial Engineers
Committee on Productivity
25 Technology Park/Atlanta
Norcross, GA 30092
(404) 449-0460

American Productivity Center
123 North Post Oak Lane
Houston, TX 77024
(713) 681-4020

American Productivity Management Association
4711 Golf Road, Suite 412
Skokie, IL 60076
(312) 677-9141

Center for Government and Public Affairs
Auburn University
Montomery, AL 36117
(205) 279-9110

Center for Manufacturing Productivity and Technology Transfer
Jonsson Engineering Center
Rensselaer Polytechnic Institute
Troy, NY 12181
(518) 270-6000

Center for Productive Public Management
John Jay College of Criminal Justice
City University of New York
445 West 59th Street
New York, NY 10019
(212) 489-5030

Center for Productivity and Quality of Work Life
Utah State University, UMC 35
Logan, UT 84322
(801) 752-4100

Center for Productivity Studies
Kogod College of Business Administration
The American University
Washington, DC 20016
(202) 686-2149

**Center for Quality of Working
  Life**
Pennsylvania State University
Capitol Campus
Middletown, PA 17057
(717) 787-7746

**Center for Quality of Working
  Life**
Institute of Industrial Relations,
  UCLA
405 Hilgard Avenue
Los Angeles, CA 90024
(213) 825-1095

Computer Integrated Design
Manufacturing and Automation
  Center
Purdue University—Grissom Hall
West Lafayette, IN 49707
(317) 494-1455

Georgia Productivity Center
Georgia Tech Engineering
  Experiment Station
Atlanta, GA 30332
(404) 894-3404

The John Gray Institute
Lamar University
P.O. Box 10067
Beaumont, TX 77710
(713) 838-8955

**Harvard Project on Technology
  Work and Character**
1710 Connecticut Avenue, N.W.
Washington, DC 20009
(202) 462-3003

Hospital Productivity Center
Texas Hospital Association
P.O. Box 15587
Austin, TX 78761
(512) 453-7204

Japan Productivity Center
1001 Connecticut Avenue, N.W.
Suite 78
Washington, DC 20036
(202) 331-1533

**Laboratory for Manufacturing
  and Productivity**
Massachusetts Institute of
  Technology, Room 35-136
Cambridge, MA 02139
(617) 253-2225

**Management and Behavioral
  Science Center**
Wharton School
University of Pennsylvania
3733 Spruce Street
Philadelphia, PA 19174
(215) 243-5736

**Manufacturing Productivity
  Center**
IIT Center
10 West 35th Street
Chicago, IL 60616
(312) 567-4800

**Maryland Center for Productivity
  and Quality of Work Life**
University of Maryland
College Park, MD 20742
(301) 454-6688

**Michigan Quality of Work Life
  Council**
6560 Cass Avenue, Suite 315
Detroit, MI 48202
(313) 871-3490

**National Association of
  Suggestion Systems**
230 North Michigan Avenue
Chicago, IL 60601
(312) 372-1770

National Center for Public Productivity
John Jay College of Criminal Justice
445 West 59th Street
New York, NY 10019
(212) 489-5030

Northeast Labor-Management Center
30 Church Street
Boston, MA 02178
(617) 489-4002

Oklahoma Productivity Center
Engineering North
Oklahoma State University
Stillwater, OK 74078
(405) 624-6055

Oregon Productivity Center
100 Merryfield Hall
Oregon State University
Corvallis, OR 97331
(503) 754-3249

Pennsylvania Technical Assistance Program
J. Orvis Keller Building
University Park, PA 16802
(814) 865-0427

Productivity Center
Chamber of Commerce of the United States
1615 H Street, N.W.
Washington, DC 20062
(202) 659-3163

Productivity Center
Graduate School of Business
Northwestern University
Evanston, IL 60201
(312) 492-3465

The Productivity Center
University of Miami
P.O. Box 248294
Coral Gables, FL 33124
(305) 284-2344

Productivity Council of the Southwest
5151 State University Drive, STF 124
Los Angeles, CA 90032
(312) 224-2975

Productivity Evaluation Center
Virginia Tech
302 Whitmore Hall
Blacksburg, VA 24061
(703) 961-6656

Productivity Group
Hartford Graduate Center
275 Windsor Street
Hartford, CT 06120
(203) 549-3600

Productivity Information Center
National Technical Information Service
425 Thirteenth Street, N.W., Suite 620
Washington, DC 20004
(202) 724-3369

Productivity Institute
College of Business Administration
Arizona State University
Tempe, AZ 85281
(602) 965-7626

Productivity Research and Extension Program
North Carolina State University
P.O. Box 5511
Raleigh, NC 27607
(919) 733-2370

Purdue Productivity Center
School of Industrial Engineering
Purdue University
West Lafayette, IN 47907
(317) 494-1455

Quality of Work Life Program
Ohio State University
1375 Perry Street
Columbus, OH 43201
(614) 422-3390

Quality of Working Life Program
Institute of Labor and Industrial
Relations
University of Illinois at Urbana
504 Eastarmoury Avenue
Champaign, IL 61820
(217) 333-0981

**State Government Productivity
Research Center**
Council of State Governments
P.O. Box 11910
Lexington, KY 40578
(606) 252-2291

**Texas Center for Productivity
and Quality of Work Life**
Texas Tech University
P.O. Box 4320
Lubbock, TX 74909
(806) 742-1538

**Utah State University Center for
Productivity and Quality of
Working Life**
Utah State University, UMC 35
Logan, UT 84322
(801) 750-1000

Work in America Institute
700 White Plains Road
Scarsdale, NY 10583
(914) 472-9600

Companies with Active Productivity or Quality-of-Work-Life Programs

Air Products & Chemicals, Inc.
Allentown, PA

Allen-Bradley Company
Milwaukee, WI

Allis-Chalmers Manufacturing Co.
Milwaukee, WI

Allstate Insurance Co.
Northbrook, IL

American Express Company
New York, NY

American Can Company
Greenwich, CT

American Hospital Supply Corp.
Evanston, IL

Anheuser-Busch, Inc.
St. Louis, MO

Armco Incorporated
Middletown, OH

Babcock & Wilcox Company
New Orleans, LA

Beatrice Foods Company
Chicago, IL

Becton-Dickinson & Company
Rutherford, NJ

Boise Cascade Corporation
Boise, ID

Boston Edison Company
Boston, MA

Bristol-Myers Company
New York, NY

Brown & Root Company
Houston, TX

Celanese Chemical Company, Inc.
Dallas, TX

Central Bancshares
Birmingham, AL

Cities Service Company
Tulsa, OK

The Continental Corporation
Neptune, NJ

Control Data Corporation
Minneapolis, MN

Dayco Corporation
Waynesville, NC

Detroit Edison Company
Detroit, MI

Emerson Electric
St. Louis, MO

Employee Transfer Corporation
Chicago, IL

Ethical, Inc.
Somerville, NJ

First City National Bank
Houston, TX

FMC Corporation
Chicago, IL

GTE Automatic Electric, Inc
Northlake, IL

General Electric Company
Fairfield, CT

General Mills, Inc.
Minneapolis, MN

General Motors Corporation
Warren, MI

General Telephone & Electronic, Corp.
Stamford, CT

Gould Incorporated
Rolling Meadows, IL

Gruman Aerospace Corporation
Bethpage, NY

Hazeltine Corporation
Greenlawn, NY

Hoffman-La Roche, Inc.
Nutley, NJ

Honeywell, Incorporated
Minneapolis, MN

Huron Machine Products, Inc.
Fort Lauderdale, FL

IBM Corporation
Armonk, NY

Intel Corporation
Santa Clara, CA

S.C. Johnson & Son Corporation
Racine, WI

Joy Manufacturing
Pittsburgh, PA

Lear-Siegler Incorporated
Santa Monica, CA

Litton Industries
Woodland Hills, CA

McDonnell Douglas Automation Co.
St. Louis, MO

Marriot Corporation
Washington, DC

Mattel Toys
Hawthorne, PA

Mead Corporation
Dayton, OH

Merck & Company, Inc.
Rahway, NJ

Miles Laboratories, Inc.
Elkhart, IN

Nabisco, Inc.
East Hanover, NJ

Olin Corporation
Stamford, CT

PET Incorporated
St. Louis, MO

Phillips Petroleum Company
Bartlesville, OK

Raytheon Company
Lexington, MA

Robbins & Meyers, Inc.
Dayton, OH

Rockwell International Corp.
Downey, Ca

Sangamo Weston-
Schlumberger
West Union, SC

Signode Corporation
Glenview, IL

Syntex Corporation
Palo Alto, CA

Tenneco, Inc.
Houston, TX

Toledo Edison Company
Toledo, OH

TRW, Incorporated
Cleveland, OH

United Technologies Corporation
Hartford, CT

Warner-Lambert Company
Morris Plains, NJ

A Selected Bibliography

Abernathy, William J. *The Productivity Dilemma: Roadblock to Innovation in the Automobile Industry.* Baltimore: Johns Hopkins, 1978.

Adam, Everett E., Jr., James C. Hershauer, and William A. Ruch, "Measuring the Quality Dimension of Service Productivity." National Science Foundation Grant #APR 76-07140, 1977.

Adkins, Lynn. "Getting a Grip on White Collar Productivity," *Dunne's Review,* December, 1979.

"AIRCO's New Approach to White Collar Productivity," *Modern Office Procedures,* October, 1980, pp. 186–192.

Allen, Fred J. "Ways to Improve Employee Communications," *Nations Business,* September, 1975.

Alter, Stephen L. *Decision Support Systems: Current Practices and Continuing Challenges.* Menlo Park, CA: Addison-Wesley, 1978.

The American Assembly. *Capital For Productivity In Jobs.* Englewood Cliffs, N.J.: Prentice-Hall, 1977.

American Productivity Center. *Inflation and Unemployment: The Productivity Solution.* Houston, Texas: American Productivity Center.

American Productivity Center. *Productivity Perspectives: A Chartbook of Key Factors About U.S. and Worldwide Productivity Trends.* Houston, Texas: American Productivity Center, 1980.

Bair, James H. "Communication in the Offices of the Future: Where the Real Pay-off May Be." *Business Communications Review,* Jan.–Feb., 1979, pp. 3–11.

Ballantyne, Duncan. *Improving Local Government Productivity.* New York: Center for Productive Public Management, 1977.

Benton, L. B. "Application of Labor Standards to Typing Tasks," *Industrial Engineering,* October, 1977.

Bodoff, John. "The Effects of Innovation on Productivity in the Service Industries." National Science Foundation Grant # RDA 75-20597 AO1, NITS, PB 247-722, August 1975.

Booz-Allen. *Multi Client Study of Managerial/Professional Productivity,* 1980.

Burnham, Donald. *Productivity Improvement.* New York: Columbia Press, 1973.

Canning, Richard G. "Educating Executives in New Technology," *EDP Analyzer,* November, 1980.

Canning, Richard G. "Getting Ready for Managerial Work Stations," *EDP Analyzer,* Dec. 1980.

Cannon, Bernard W. "New Frontiers in Productivity Improvement: White Collar Workers," *Industrial Engineering,* December, 1979.

Craig, Charles E., and R. Clark Harris. "Total Productivity Measurement at the Firm Level," *Sloane Management Review,* Spring, 1973.

Crane, Edward G. et al, *State Government Productivity: The Environment For Improvement.* New York: Praeger, 1976.

Cummings, Thomas G., and Edmund S. Malloy. *Improving Productivity and Quality of Work Life.* New York: Praeger, 1977.

Dahl, Henry L., Jr. "Measuring the Human ROI," *Management Review,* January, 1979, pp. 44–50.

Dallas, Daniel B. "New Insights into Productivity," *Manufacturing Engineering,* December, 1979.

Davis, Hiran. *Productivity Accounting.* Philadelphia: University of Pennsylvania, The Wharton School, Reprint edition, 1978.

Drucker, Peter F. "Managing the Knowledge Worker," *Wall Street Journal,* Nov. 7, 1975.

"Electronic Mail: Technology Adds Speedy Options to Communications," *Houston Business Journal,* Dec. 29, 1980, p. 5.

Fabricant, Solomon. *A Primer of Productivity.* New York: Random House, 1971.

Gale, Bradley T. "How to Establish Productivity Benchmarks," Strategic Planning Institute, Cambridge MA, January, 1980.

Gale, Bradley T. "Balancing Capital and Labor Productivity," October, 1979.

Gardner, Howard. "On Becoming a Dictator," *Psychology Today,* December, 1980, pp. 14–19.

Greenberg, H.D. et al. "Productivity Measurement Systems for Administrative Services: Computing and Information Services," National Science Foundation Grant #APR 75-20546, 1977.

Greenberg, Leon. *A Practical Guide to Productivity Measurement.* Washington, DC: BNA Books, 1973.

Gregerman, Ira B. "Construction Site Productivity Measurement Using Work Sampling," *Transactions, American Association of Cost Engineers,* 25th Annual meeting, Toronto, Canada, July 1981.

Gregerman, Ira B. "Knowledge Worker Productivity: Characteristics and Measures," *Transactions, American Association of Cost Engineers,* 25th Annual Meeting, Toronto, Canada, July, 1981.

Gregerman, Ira B. "Knowledge Worker Productivity Measurement Through the Nominal Group Technique," *Industrial Management,* Jan.–Feb., 1981, V. 23, n. 1, p. 5.

Gregerman, Ira B. "Productivity—A Challenge to Be Met," *I & NS Journal,* Iron & Steel Society, V. 7, n. 2, February, 1980.

Gregerman, Ira B. "White Collar Productivity and the Nominal Group Technique," *Productivity,* V. 1, n. 3, August, 1980.

Gregerman, Ira B. "Introduction to Quality Circles: An Approach to Participative Problem Solving," *Industrial Management,* Sept.–Oct., 1979, V. 21, n. 5.

Gregerman, Ira B. et al. *How to Involve Employees In Productivity Improvement.* Houston, Texas: American Productivity Center, 1979.

Haskell, Deborah L. "White Collar Productivity: Management's No. 1 Concern," *Modern Office Procedures,* September, 1979, pp. 40–46.

Hornbruch, F. W., Jr. *Raising Productivity.* New York: McGraw-Hill, 1977.

Jacobs, Herman S., with Katherine Jillson, *Executive Productivity,* AMA Survey Report, ANACOM, 1974.

Johansen, Robert. *Electronic Meetings: Technical Alternatives and Social Choices.* Menlo Park, CA: Addison-Wesley Publishing Co., 1979.

Katzell, Mildred E. *Productivity: The Measure and the Myth.* AMA Survey Report, AMACOM, 1975.

Katzell, Raymond. *A Guide to Work with Productivity Experiments in the United States,* 1971–1975. New York: New York University Press, 1971.

Katzell, Raymond. *Work, Productivity and Job Satisfaction: An Evaluation of Policy Related Research.* New York: Harcourt Brace Jovanovich, 1975.

Katzen, Raphael. "Measuring the Productivity of Engineers," *Chemical Engineering Progress,* April, 1975.

Kendrick, John W. *Postwar Productivity Trends in the United States,* 1948–1969. New York: National Bureau of Economic Research, 1973.

Kendrick, John W. *Understanding Productivity.* Baltimore, Md.: The Johns Hopkins University Press, 1977.

Kendrick, J.W. & D. Creamer. *Measuring Company Productivity: Handbook with Case Studies.* Studies in Business Economics, #44, New York: The Conference Board, 1961.

Kerr, E. D. *Productivity in U.S. Railroads.* New York: Pergamon, 1979.

Killian, Ray. *Human Resource Management: An ROI Approach.* AMACOM New York, 1976.

Lester, Tom. "The Office Conundrum," *Management Today,* November, 1978, pp. 116–117.

McBeath, Maurice. *Productivity Through People.* New York: Wiley 1974.

Mali, Paul. *Improving Total Productivity: MBO Strategies for Business, Government and Not for Profit Organizations.* New York: Wiley-Interscience, 1978.

Mason, Anthony K. *Improving Productivity in the Courts.* Washington, DC: U.S. Government Printing Office. Stock # 027-000-00677-9.

Mathein, Daniel J. "Creative Decision Making—An Overview," 44th Annual IMS Proceedings, November 1980, p. 190.

"Measuring Performance of Accounting and Management Personnel," *CPA Journal,* February 1978, pp. 81–85.

Merrill, Peter, and T. Krishna Kumar. "Productivity Measurement & the Budget & Management Control Function," National Science Foundation Grant # APR 75-20564, 1977.

Meyer, John. *Improving Urban Mass Transportation Productivity.* Cambridge: Harvard University Press, 1977.

Miller, Donald B. "How to Improve the Performance and Productivity of the Knowledge Worker," *Organizational Dynamics,* Winter, 1977, pp. 62–79.

Monezka, Robert M., and Philip L. Cotter. "Productivity Measurement Systems for Administrative Services: Purchasing," National Science Foundation Grant No. APR 75-20557 1977.

Moore, Brian, and Ross, T. L. *The Scanlon Way to Improved Productivity: A Practical Guide.* New York: Wiley Interscience, 1978.

Morris, William M., and Scott Sink. "Measuring and Improving the Productivity of Administrative Computing and Information Services," National Science Foundation Grant # APR 75-20561.

Mundel, Marvin E. *Productivity: A Series from Industrial Engineering.* Norcross, Ga: American Institute of Industrial Engineers, 1978.

National Science Foundation. *Industrial Productivity,* Two Volumes, 1976.

Norman, R. G., and S. Bahiri. *Productivity Measurement & Incentives.* London: Butterworth's, 1972.

"Now the Office of Tomorrow," *Time Magazine,* November 17, 1980, pp. 80–82.

O'Dell, Carla S. *Gainsharing: Involvement, Incentives and Productivity.* New York: AMACOM, 1981.

"Office of the Future," *CPA Journal,* February, 1980 p. 77–80.

Ohio State University, Productivity Research Group. *Productivity Measurement Systems for Administrative, Computing & Information Services.* Washington, D.C.: U.S. Department of Commerce, National Technical Information Service, 1977, PB-292698.

Peeples, Donald E. "Measure for Productivity," *Datamation,* May, 1978.

Plonka, Francis E. "A Productivity Measurement System for State and Local Government Purchasing and Materials Management Services," National Science Foundation Grant # APR 75-20542 1977.

Presnick, Walter J. "Measuring Managerial Productivity," *Administrative Management,* May, 1980, pp. 26–28.

Productivity Agreement, Worker Motivation and Sharing the Gains of Productivity. New York: Unipub, 1978.

Resow, Jerome. "Public Sector Pay and Productivity," *Harvard Business Review,* January–February, 1977.

R & D Productivity, Second Edition. Culver City, Calif.: Hughes Aircraft Co., 1978.

Rhodes, Wayne L., Jr. "Office of the Future: Fact or Fantasy?" *Infosystems,* March, 1980, p. 45.

Ross, Joel E. *Managing Productivity.* Reston, Va: 1977.

Ross, John P., and Jesse Burkhead. *Productivity in the Local Government Sector.* Lexington, Mass: Lexington Books, 1974.

Ruch, William A. "Measuring Knowledge Worker Productivity," Paper presented at the Conference on Productivity Research sponsored by the American Productivity Center, April 20–24, 1980, Houston, Texas.

Ruch, William A., Everett E. Adam, Jr., and James C. Hershauer. "Quality Measures for Bank Operations," *Bank Administration,* July, 1979.

Ruch, William A., and James C. Hershauer. "Factors Affecting Worker Productivity." Arizona State University, 1974.

Rudge, Frederick. *The Key to Increased Productivity.* Washington, D.C.: Bureau of National Affairs, 1977.

Salter, W. E. *Productivity & Technical Change.* Cambridge: Cambridge University Press, 1966.

Scheppach, Raymond C. *Transportation Productivity: Measurement and Policy Applications.* Lexington, Mass.: Lexington Books, 1975.

Scott, Robert C. "Production Sharing Incentive Programs: Are They for You?" *Furniture Design and Manufacturing,* March, 1977.

Shore, John Clark. *The Quality—Productivity Connection in Service—Sector Management.* New York: Van Nostrand Reinhold, 1978.

Sloma, Richard. *How to Measure Managerial Performance.* New York: Macmillan, 1980.

Sowards, Dennis. "Marketing Productivity: An Effort in Measurement," *Harvest,* March, 1978.

Srivastra, Suresh, et al. *Job Satisfaction & Productivity! An Evaluation of Policy Related Research on Productivity, Industrial Organization & Job Satisfaction.* Kent, Ohio: Kent State University Press, 1977.

U. S. Bureau of Labor Statistics. *Productivity and the Economy.* Washington, D.C.: U.S. Printing Office, 1977. Bulletin # 1926.

U. S. Bureau of Labor Statistics. *Productivity Indexes for Selected Industries,* 1980 edition. Washington, D.C.: U.S. Government Printing Office, 1980.

Van Niekerk, W. P. *Productivity and Work Study.* Durban: Butterworth, 1978.

Vough, Clair F. *Productivity: A Practical Program Through Improving Efficiency.* New York: AMACOM, 1979.

Vough, Clair F. *Tapping the Human Resource: A Strategy for Productivity.* New York: AMA, 1975.

Washnis, George J. *Productivity Improvement Handbook for State and Local Government.* New York: Wiley, 1979.

Wilkinson, Joseph W. "The Meaning of Measurements," *Management Accounting,* July, 1975.

Wolfe, Joan, and John F. Heaphy, eds. *Readings on Productivity in Policing.* Washington, D.C.: Police Foundation, 1975.

Zintara, Marguerite. "Productivity Peg to Office Automation," *Computerworld,* May 5, 1980, p. 1.

Index